Other Books by David Lemon

Ivory Madness :	College Press, Harare 1983
Africa's Inland Sea:	Modus Press 1987
Kariba Adventure:	College Press 1988
Rhino:	Puffin Books 1989
Man Eater:	Viking Books 1990
Hobo Rows Kariba:	African Publishing Group 1997
Killer Cat:	College Press 1998
Never Quite a Soldier:	Albida Books 2000
Never Quite a Soldier:	(South African Edition) Galago Books 2006.

Blood Sweat and Lions

by

David Lemon

Grosvenor House
Publishing Limited

This book is published by
Grosvenor House Publishing Ltd
28-30 High Street, Guildford, Surrey, GU1 3HY.
www.grosvenorhousepublishing.co.uk

A CIP record for this book
is available from the British Library

ISBN 978-1-906210-66-3

Acknowledgements

Although I walked from Kariba Town to Binga on my own, it was hardly a solo achievement as many folk made it possible in one way or another. I have mentioned some of them in the text, but to everyone who assisted in any way, I will be eternally grateful. Some – even apart from my 'Angel of Chalala' – deserve a very special mention, so to -

Moses and Elizabeth Shumbirai who started me off so well; Geoff and Nikki Blyth who were always there for me: Dollar Karingaramambo whose assistance was enthusiastic and his mentor whose encouragement kept me going when my spirits were low: Ursula Smith who was on the end of a phone on the rare occasions I could get through: my oldest friend Mervyn Rollinson; Louise Walker, Stuart Lacey and of course Bushpig, Janice and Sean Kok who helped put me back together when it was all over - without your help, I could not have succeeded.

I should also thank Glyn Hunter, Kathryn Burgoyne and Hilda Olivier, three lovely ladies in different parts of the world, whose prayers for my safety undoubtedly stood me in good stead and were a great comfort at all times.

My family, the Falkenbergs and a few – a very few – of my friends deserve a special mention for not scoffing when they heard about my plans. Audrey McGeorge even enthused about the idea, which was a big lift to my spirits. My long-suffering agent, Frances Bond puts up with so much from me, yet even she didn't quibble when her not-very-successful investment wandered off again into the wide blue yonder. My daughter in law Gillian deserves a special medal for ploughing through the text and smartening up the pictures in this book.

There were many others who assisted in one way or another and if I have not mentioned them by name, I am sorry but they can rest assured that they have not been forgotten and have my sincere gratitude.

This one is for
Lace to make up for a lot.

Introduction

'You are too old - it is a ridiculous idea - you will have a heart attack - a stroke - you are cooked in the head.' All these and more were thrown at me when I announced my intention to walk from Kariba Town to Binga along the southern shoreline of Lake Kariba in northern Zimbabwe.

It was indeed an ambitious project and something that had never been attempted before but I am no stranger to adventure in Africa. When I was in my forties, I rowed an open dinghy over a thousand kilometres from one end of Lake Kariba to the other and back again. They told me I was too old then but many younger folk have tried it before and since, only to fail and on occasion lose their lives in that unforgiving water. In my fifties I cycled seven and a half thousand kilometres from Nairobi to Cape Town. Before I started out, they told me I was too old but four and a half months later, I made it. Walking the lakeshore would be an enormous physical challenge and at sixty-one, of course I was too old. But why was everyone so worried.

'You are mad. You will kill yourself and nobody will ever know. How will you cope with the heat – a bad fall – a puff adder bite?' The warnings came from around the world and even my friend Geoff Blyth, who lives in Kariba and knows the bush as well as I do was scathingly dismissive. It was when Geoff described my proposed adventure as 'gung ho' that I became seriously determined to do the walk, whatever it might cost me.

Gung ho indeed! My little adventures are done for my own sake and I am not out to impress anyone. Risking my life in wild surroundings from time to time seems to assuage some atavistic instinct in me and is necessary to keep my soul in working order. I have never considered myself in any way 'gung ho.'

My children understand this and my younger son expressed acute disappointment that he couldn't join me on the trip. His home is in Australia and he has a young family to consider so although Graeme is one person I could possibly adventure with, I was glad he didn't push the matter. The other two, accustomed to their father's occasional eccentricities, merely shrugged their shoulders and wished me luck. Lace hasn't been married to me long enough to truly understand my odd urges to do something different, but she gave me her full support and joined in my preparations with her usual good-humoured practicality.

But still the objections flooded in.

'What about lions?' They said. 'What about elephant, buffalo, hyena, hippopotamus and crocodiles? You will die a violent death out there and nobody will know what has happened to you.'

It was undoubtedly possible and a risk that I needed to consider, but I grew up with lions, elephant, buffaloes et al. I respect dangerous wild life but have always felt safer among such creatures than I do while crossing the road in towns or cities. Besides, I knew the area well.

I have spent a great deal of my life on wonderful Lake Kariba. Situated on the northern border of Zimbabwe, it is the fifth largest man-made lake in the world and undoubtedly the wildest and most remote. Set right in the middle of the Zambezi Valley, it is a haven for wild life and in the halcyon days of tourism in Zimbabwe, Kariba was a Mecca for visitors from all over the world. They came to marvel at the savagely rugged terrain around the lake, to watch dangerous wild animals in their natural surroundings and to shiver in fear at their proximity to massively built crocodiles.

For me it is merely home. I have lived in Kariba Town for many years. I have sailed into some of the more remote reaches of its six thousand square kilometre expanse and rowed it in my beloved dinghy, Hobo. I have swum in its waters on many occasions and still drink them quite happily - much to the horror of ever more health-conscious Zimbabweans. I have sat spell-bound through Kariba sunsets and fiery dawns and I have trembled in terror at the mercy of its storms. I know and understand that vast stretch of water better than most folk and I love the local inhabitants – the peaceful Tonga people who eke out a precariously primitive exis-tence as fishermen and hunter/gatherers along the lakeshore. They have little in the way of possessions or material wealth, but they are so very hospitable and have hearts as big as Africa itself.

In view of the time I have spent on and around Lake Kariba, it seemed somehow fitting that it should provide the focus for what might well be my last real adventure. After all, I am far too old for any more – I think.

So why walk to Binga? Since I first mooted the idea at the beginning of 2006 I have been asked that question on numerous occasions and in truth, I do not know the answer. 'Because it is there,' sounds too glib and besides, there has to be a deeper reason behind my venture. I have brooded on the potential challenge for years and my original intention was to walk right around the lake – a journey that is officially calculated at two thousand four hundred and fifty kilometres. The drawback to that however was that firstly, it would take me about eight months and I did not have that amount of time to spare. Secondly, two countries and the corresponding border crossings would be involved, so I would need to carry my passport and would have to pay visa fees etc. I know Africa far too well and did not want the hassles and frustration offered by petty officialdom. This walk was to be enjoyed.

So I decided to split my walk into two halves. I would do the southern part in 2006, rest a year and then walk the Zambian side. It all seemed delightfully simple and studying the map, I decided that although I would be walking well over half the total circumference of the lake in my first foray, I ought to be able to complete it in three months.

It really would be 'a walk on the wild side' though. That southern shoreline has little habitation, few roads and is known for its rugged terrain and the man-eating propensities of its lions. It could prove interesting.

Getting out afterwards might prove a problem but Binga has a fairly substantial community and an economic infrastructure of sorts. I had friends there who would be happy to put me up if I survived the walk. I would have no difficulty in getting a bus from Binga to Bulawayo and making my way from there to Harare, so Binga Town seemed the logical place to end my walk.

The physical part of the venture would be a mighty challenge. Officially, it would entail walking some eleven hundred and eighty kilometres and with the drastic drop in the lake level that occurred in 2005, this could turn out to be considerably more. I thought I could manage it.

Having made up my mind that if I didn't do the walk in 2006, I would never do it, I ignored all the warnings and started planning my trip. I was overweight and not very fit, but that would soon be remedied.

Lace and I run a gardening business, so I took on ever more heavy jobs, while tramping the steep hills of Gloucestershire with a pack full of books on my back. Gym work was suggested, but I have an inbuilt horror of such activities and relied on getting fit as I went along – a policy that has always sufficed in the past. I would start off slowly and the walk should become easier as my strength and fitness built up. That was the theory at any rate.

A big problem was when to start. March to September is a busy time for English gardeners, but not for nothing is October known as suicide month in Zimbabwe. That is when the heat builds up and the humidity increases before the onset of the rains. In Kariba and the Zambezi Valley, this would be exacerbated by the low altitude and although I have always boasted that I can take either heat or cold, my ability to withstand high temperatures was going to be sorely tested.

It was suggested that I postpone my start until the rains set in, but I know from experience that with a bit of rain, the bush takes very little time to thicken up and I had to take advantage of at least a few weeks when the going was relatively easy and the mosquitoes were still resting up for the winter. Besides, starting toward the end of October, I would experience the delights of early

showers and witness the mass birth of impala fawns –
always a fascinating few days.

I intended to stay reasonably close to the lake anyway,
so water would not prove a problem for me – or so I
thought.

Food was a major worry. I was giving myself three
months to complete the walk but would have to carry
everything on my back. I could probably supplement my
diet with fish from the lake, but that meant carrying a
hand line and the necessary tackle. I spent many hours
practicing with a catapult in case I met up with the occasional suicidal game bird or rabbit – even a rock hyrax
would do - but there was always an irritating little doubt
in the back of my mind. I have never been a fisherman
and I am extremely squeamish when it comes to skinning
and gutting anything. Besides, I do not enjoy killing,
although I supposed that if it was necessary to keep
myself alive, I wouldn't hesitate. In the event, I left my
catapult behind and although I took a variety of fishing
gear, it remained unused until it was eventually given
away to a grateful Tonga boatman.

So what was I going to eat? Walking that sort of
distance over brutally rough terrain and in searing heat
was going to take a great deal out of me, so I needed
sustenance. I know nothing about calories, kilojoules or
proteins but I did know that I had to have plenty of nourishment if I was to survive.

I was in the dried foods section of a local supermarket one afternoon when I spotted what appeared to be
the ideal food for my purpose. 'Meal in a Mug' the label
proclaimed proudly and the packet itself was very small
and light. As far as I could see, the ingredients consisted
of chicken and mushroom soup with pasta, so I took

some home to try. The 'meal in a mug' tasted splendid, so every supermarket visit from then on meant buying twenty or so of the damned things until I had just over a hundred. I would be too hot and sweaty for hunger anyway, so was sure I could make do with one meal a day. There were only four or five flavours to these meals, but they all contained pasta so would surely supply me with sufficient nourishment. I supplemented them with packets of tiny 'fruit flakes' and felt I could not only carry the whole lot of them but could survive on the sustenance they provided.

I should have paid more attention to the small print.

Kit was relatively easy to sort out. I already possessed a pair of sturdily hand-made, Zimbabwean Courteney boots which were ideal for the purpose and would afford some protection against puff adders. I purchased a ninety-litre backpack on Ebay, some durable shorts and items of camp equipment from an outdoor shop, a compass and water bags from the same source and I was ready to roll. I even had a bush jacket, guaranteed to keep me cool in the hottest conditions – it didn't – and a hat that would keep insects away, ensure that my head was cool at all times and do everything but play God save the Queen and tell me which way to go. I lost faith in the hat when I saw two flies engaged in earnest discussion while sitting happily and quite unharmed on the brim. Still it was fun. Lace bought me an expensively rugged Leatherman tool as a combined birthday and Christmas (I would be away for both) present and I picked up a few more exotics like a wind up torch, similarly powered phone charger and solar battery charger from various sources.

My first aid kit seemed akin to a small hospital and for entertainment, I would have a small digital radio, lovingly given to me for the purpose. I carried a dicta-phone and of course I had my trusty camera to record the adventure in detail. In Harare, the Falkenberg family provided the finishing touches to my equipment. Paul produced a sturdy bush knife, which I honed to perfec-tion; John came up with four thunder flashes to scare off troublesome lions and Sandra gave me a long-sleeved cotton shirt that was ideal for my purpose.

I was prepared, but when I arrived in Kariba, the sheer magnitude of the task I had set myself really hit home. Standing on the high hills on which the town is situated and gazing out at the lake I felt my heart sink into my boots. The entire Eastern Basin was spread out before me, shimmering in forty-degree heat. The Matu-sadona mountains glared back across the basin and the hills of Bumi seemed half a world away. I could as easily have been looking out on a vast inland sea as a mere man-made lake.

I consoled myself with the thought that I had rowed my tiny Hobo across that enormous expanse of water, but it didn't help. This time, I was going to have to walk it and the thought was an appalling one. I tried dividing the basin up into walkable sections in my mind, but every time I looked past the park at Matusadona, my heart quailed at the distance involved.

I could cope with the heat, I could cope with the wild life, but could I manage the physical challenge of walk-ing hundreds of kilometres through the harsh African bush? How would I get through the parks – not only Matusadona, but the vast, wild hunting area of Chete further down the lake? Officially I required permits to enter these areas but when I had contacted the Department of National Parks and Wild Life Management in Harare, they told me that permits would have to be obtained from the respective park wardens. My protest that to reach the wardens, I would have to traverse almost the entire park in both instances was ignored. This was Africa, rules were rules and only the relevant wardens could give me permission. I would just have to get through those areas without permission – probably not a sensible idea but I felt it was the easiest way of avoiding endless expensive formalities. Besides, I wasn't sure that permission would be given, even if I did things the proper way.

Then there was the sweltering October heat. How would I cope with that? How would I cope with the rough terrain, the thick bush, lions, hyenas, crocodiles and other possibly hostile residents of the area? I didn't know and my heart sank at the prospect.

And this was only one end of the lake. After Bumi, I would have the mighty Sengwa Basin to face and then the badlands of Sinamwenda, Ruziruhuru and Chete where I knew from experience that the going would be awfully tough and lions were plentiful.

It was in a thoughtfully sombre mood that I turned away from that spectacular view and headed for the nearest bar. I was reasonably fit and have always been physically strong. I could cope with most eventualities so I would make it somehow.

I thought so anyway but all those well-meant warnings suddenly seemed awfully relevant and self-doubt gnawed at my mind. Perhaps I really was too old.

PART ONE

(A LONG WAY TO GO)

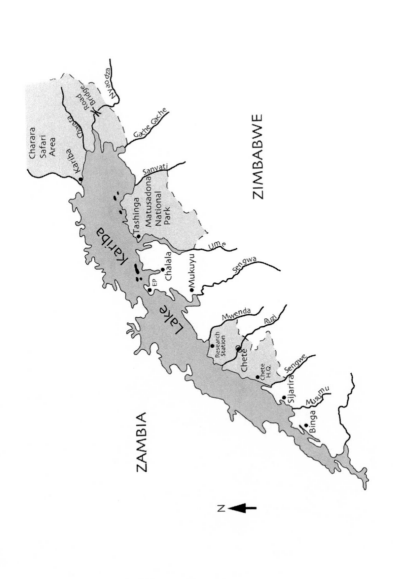

CHAPTER ONE

(Thirsty Days)

The bay was wide and very beautiful but I hardly noticed my surroundings. Glare from the mid afternoon sun reflected off the lake surface and made me screw up my eyes in pain. I had suffered from a pounding headache throughout the morning and was feeling very weak and sorry for myself. I needed food and I needed water. The heat was overpowering and water in the bay was so shallow that filling up my bottles became an enormous problem. Every time I touched the ground, silt billowed around my hands and when I tried moving into deeper water, I churned up so much of the stuff that the water looked like soup. A nearby fish eagle screamed mockingly at my frustration and I yelled at him to go away. At the sound of my voice, a goliath heron cocked his head to one side and studied me thoughtfully.

I finally managed to fill the bottle by dipping the cap carefully into clean water and pouring from there – a long, slow, laborious and hellishly hot process.

Trying to look more confident than I felt, I had left the Blyths' house the previous morning and although Binga was to the West, I had to walk due East in order to get around the huge bulge of the Eastern Basin. Already I was in trouble. I felt as though I was walking through a gigantic furnace. My skin cringed under the onslaught of the sun and even the countryside around me seemed to creak in a temperature that had been forty-four degrees when I started walking. My shirt was wringing wet and sweaty socks made it feel as though I was wading through two uncomfortable pools of dank moisture.

My back pack didn't help either. I had pared my kit down to the minimum but the pack weighed well over twenty kilograms and the broad straps tugging on my shoulders seemed to cut off the circulation from my arms and left me with a permanent tingle in my fingers. Life seemed full of acute discomfort and once again I wondered whether I had been sensible in ignoring so many well-intentioned warnings. Of course I hadn't but it was far too late to call the walk off. I was committed and would just have to make the best of things as I went along.

With my bottle full, I wandered somewhat disconsolately back to my little camp. I had laid my mattress beneath the remains of an old game-viewing platform and although it wasn't particularly comfortable, I didn't care any more. The entire venture seemed pointless and somewhat suicidal. Why was I doing this to myself? The question was unanswerable and I sat with my back against the pack and gazed out across the lake.

It was a magnificent vista but for once it did little for my soul. My legs ached and I felt unutterably weary. Two zebra stallions did battle for a group of mares only a few hundred metres from where I sat but I didn't care. I didn't think I could continue with the walk but the thought of going back to admit failure was a pretty horrific one. Those who had mocked my plans would be proved correct and although nobody would say it to my face, I knew there would be much ribald chat about my empty headedness in the pubs of Kariba. Geoff Blyth would be proved right too and I could just imagine his amusement at my failure.

No, I had to go on, but could I manage it? I didn't know and my heart was heavy. All things being equal, I felt I could reach the National Anglers' Union camp at Charara the following day and although that would give me a chance to rest and chill out a little, it would also be time to make my first major decision.

My original intention was to stick as close as possible to the lakeshore whenever I could, but to do that I would have to walk up one bank of the broad Nyaodza River and that would lead me directly through the army commando training ground at Wafa Wafa. In Chishona, the name means 'we die; we die' and I would be taking a huge risk by walking through the area. The Zimbabwean army are notorious for their hostility to strangers and no matter how careful I was, their bush craft would undoubtedly be a great deal better than mine. I certainly didn't fancy '*wafa* - ing' myself beneath the guns of trig-ger-happy soldiers.

The alternative was to take the road along the power lines, which was considerably longer and moved well away from the lake and into the hills before veering around to the Nyaodza river bridge. I knew the road well and although it crossed a few small streams and rivers, these would be dry at this time of the year so I would need to walk nearly forty kilometres with the water I had in my containers – a meagre seven litres which wouldn't go far in that searing heat.

It was an agonizing dilemma but I put it out of my mind for the moment and tried to enjoy the tranquil beauty of my surroundings.

In the event, my route was decided by my own ineptitude. After a restful day among the big trees and thick green grass of Charara, I set out just before dawn the following day, my intention being to risk military intervention and take the shorter route through Wafa Wafa. I felt that I could probably sneak through at night if necessary. With all the army activity in the area, the chance of bumping into lions would be fairly remote and I decided that if the army were about during the hours of darkness, they would be on manoeuvres and I would therefore have ample warning of their presence. Unless of course they were practising ambush drills but that would be just too bad.

Incredibly I could feel my teeth chattering with the early morning cold as I left the comforts of Charara but I knew it wouldn't last. The sky was a very pale blue and there wasn't a cloud in sight. Once the sun moved up through the morning, the heat would hammer at my mind and body once again.

Crossing the wide sandy bed of the Charara River, I moved through the empty fields and pathways of the Kariba Banana Farm and wasn't overly disturbed when I came out of some trees to find myself on the bank of the river again. I knew that the Charara twisted and turned to a marked degree in this area, so it wasn't until I hauled myself up the opposite bank and found myself almost back where I had started that I knew I had gone wrong.

I was on the power lines road whether I liked it or not, so feeling that the decision had been taken from me, I turned my face to the East and set out along that long, straight and dusty highway. Huge pylons carrying electricity to the rest of the country stretched away in two straight lines ahead of me and the Nyaodza hills looked a hazy purple in the morning light. The road moved gradually away from the lake and wondering what I was letting myself in for, I trudged into the morning.

Before leaving England, I had thought long and hard on how much water I should carry on the walk. I would be close to the lake for most of the time – I thought – but knew that there would be the occasional lengthy inland detour when water could be short. In temperatures of over forty degrees, I would get through a great deal of liquid just to keep myself alive but water is an incredibly heavy substance and I would have to carry my entire stock.

I eventually purchased three two-litre water bags, made in America and guaranteed to withstand all sorts of punishment. Made of heavy plastic, they were light, flexible and could be folded into a very small package. With the solid plastic belt bottle that I carried, it gave me a water capacity of seven litres and I felt that would have to be enough.

What I hadn't allowed for was accidents and my own lack of care and attention when packing. I had travelled only a few kilometres along that bleak power lines road when after taking a long drink and replacing the water bag back in one side pocket of my pack, it dropped with a thump on the road behind me and to my horror, split right down the seam.

It was a moment of pure panic. With a horrified yelp, I grabbed up the broken bag and tried to pour as much of the spilling water down my throat as I could manage. The precious liquid splashed down my front and provided a moment of blessed coolness but I hardly noticed it in my frenzied attempts to drink as much as I possibly could.

When the bag was empty, there was a pool of lost water in the sand at my feet and I gazed at it with a sense of sick horror in my stomach. I was down to five litres and that surely would not be enough unless I could find a pool in those dry brown hills ahead of me. That was an unlikely prospect and if I had had any sense at all, I would have turned around and headed back for the lake and a rethink on my position.

I didn't, but it was with a heavy heart and a sense of mounting trepidation that I walked on, sweat streaming down my body, its saltiness stinging the sunburn on my face and arms. Unshed tears burned against the insides of my eyelids.

By mid afternoon I was in trouble. There was no shade in those hills and although I saw a herd of beautiful sable and one massively tusked elephant bull that totally ignored me, I was too hot and too worried to appreciate their wild beauty. My throat felt as though it was centimetres deep in ground glass and my vision blurred with the strain of walking. I had a feeling of mounting panic in my chest. This was not how I had envisaged my walk from the comfort of gentle Gloucestershire. This was nightmarishly frightening.

The slopes on that road were steep in parts, but the going was relatively easy – or would have been if the weather had been cooler and the road surface in better condition. As it was, loose rocks and scree meant that I had to watch where I put my feet and be careful not to slip or fall.

There were few leaves on the trees and shade was at a premium. Spotting a solitary combretum bush on the edge of a dry ravine, I crawled into its meagre shadow and wondered what to do. I still had a good twenty-five kilometres to walk before reaching the Nyaodza bridge and I wasn't at all sure I would make it. I was sweating profusely and the more I sweated, the thirstier I became. Even when I wasn't walking, I kept taking tiny sips of water and the level of my remaining stocks was dropping fast.

The obvious answer was to walk at night when the temperature would or should be a good fifteen degrees lower. But that was a horrifying prospect. This was wild, primeval Africa, an area teeming with wild life and the possibilities of bumping into something large and dangerous in the darkness were very real. There was a little slice of moon left but it would only appear in the wee small hours so I would have to do most of the walk in total darkness. The road surface was rough and gravelly so quite apart from the dangers of wild life, I stood an excellent chance of falling or twisting an ankle during my walk.

On the other hand, I didn't think my remaining water supplies would last the night and they certainly wouldn't keep me going through the following day. The thought of walking through that crippling heat without water was an appalling one and I knew I would not survive that sort of ordeal.

I didn't seem to have a choice and tried to sleep the rest of the day away so that I would be relatively fresh when I started walking. It wasn't easy. Mopani bees and ants tormented my rest through the long afternoon hours and prospects of impending disaster revolved somewhat frantically in my mind. My sparse patch of shade shifted with the movement of the sun and I found it extremely difficult to lie comfortably or sleep.

I couldn't eat because the meals in a mug required water to prepare them, so I went hungry. It was a situation I hadn't foreseen and I bitterly cursed myself for my own lack of forethought. It seemed very likely that it was going to get me killed.

There is little I can say about that long, horrible walk through the night. I did manage to doze for a few hours soon after sunset and woke feeling gummy eyed and anything but rested. Allowing myself a sip of water to wash my mouth out, I moved gingerly out on to the road and headed for the Nyaodza and many hours of frightened misery.

The sky was incredibly beautiful with a vast, shimmering expanse of cold white stars, stark against a pitch-black background that seemed to pulse with life of its own. It is a sight that is commonplace to African people but a rare one indeed for residents of the Northern hemisphere and in spite of my discomfort, it felt good to be home.

The occasional meteorite flashed across the heavens and the bush around me seemed alive with life, although the night was very quiet. Foraging hyena whooped in the distance and the sound made me shiver with anxiety, even though I knew that any hyenas were likely to give me a wide berth. I spent almost ten minutes asking an elephant beside the road to 'please move on' but when it remained perfectly still, I ventured forward a few steps only to find that I had been addressing a vaguely elephant-shaped bush. That made me smile somewhat wryly at my own idiocy but there were few other moments of levity during that long, hard night.

At one point, I disturbed something large and heard heavy hoofs clattering across rocks, but I think most wild denizens of my nocturnal world heard me coming from a long way off and moved gently away. Occasional mosquitoes whined hopefully around my face but when I swatted them away they left me alone and the night became a question of putting one foot carefully in front of the other and concentrating on the dimly seen road surface in front of me. The pack pressed heavily on my back but at that stage it was the least of my worries.

Hour after hour passed and the level of water in my containers dropped steadily. I didn't dare look at my watch and my mind almost seemed to close down in my misery. I kept myself occupied with thoughts of that wonderful river I was getting closer to with every painful step.

I have spent many happy times on the Nyaodza. As the nearest major river to Kariba town, it has always been a favourite place for picnics and family days out. My children had frequently swum in its cool water and I had seen the river in all its moods. I had marvelled at its power when in raging flood, I had seen it flowing gently as a river should and I had seen it as nothing but a series of pools with tiny trickles linking them together. Walking blindly along that rocky road, I remembered the taste of that wonderful river, drifted through hazy memories of parties beside the road bridge and imagined myself lying on my back in a cool wet pool of Nyaodza water. Somehow it kept me going.

I was almost surprised by the dawn. I suppose it must have been getting lighter by the moment, but I hadn't noticed it. Suddenly, I could see the world around me and looked anxiously for familiar landmarks that would tell where I was and how far I had to go. All I could see was dry brown bush and that horrible road stretching ahead into the distance. I wondered whether I had made any progress at all.

The sun was high in the sky when I came to a downward slope that definitely looked familiar. It curved gently away from me so that I couldn't see what was at the bottom, but my pace increased and I almost stumbled my way down that rocky hill. Suddenly there it was. I could see the road bridge with its familiar kink in the middle and I let out a small shout of triumph. I had done it. I had survived that terrible night. Now I could relax. Now I could drink without worrying about how much water I used up.

Savouring the moment, I stepped out on to the bridge and looked upstream. The river was completely dry. Brown sand, vaguely discoloured in places stretched away from the bridge before disappearing around a bend in the stream. Years ago I had christened that spot Albida Bend for the two big *acacia albida* trees that stood on either side of the river. It had been beautiful then but now it just looked hot and terribly uninviting. Downstream, the riverbed looked even dryer.

My initial reaction was pure panic. What was I going to do? I felt sick, weary and desperately old. Frightened too, because water was essential if I was to survive my little adventure that was beginning to look ever more foolish. I only had a few sips left in my bottle, but after wandering upstream in a fruitless search for the pools that ought to have been there, I came back to the road feeling very sorry for myself and found a small spring of beautifully clear water right under the road bridge itself. For a few long moments, I didn't know whether to laugh or cry. My walk could go on. I wasn't going to die of thirst in this outlandish spot.

I was terribly tired though and decided to spend that day beneath the bridge then go downstream the following day and see if I could find the lake. I didn't know how far away that might be, as I had never bothered to explore in that direction. The upper reaches of the river had always seemed more inviting. Besides I had never expected to find myself in this sort of a predicament.

It was desperately hot, my body ached abominably and my mind longed for sleep. Somehow I had to survive the next few weeks and put more than a thousand kilometres behind me. It seemed an impossible prospect but I no longer had a choice, so closed my eyes and tried to relax.

My left boot was showing a slight split between the sole and the uppers and this was still my first week! On the other hand, no matter how damaged they were, the boots would probably outlast me. It was my second day on the Nyaodza and although I had started out at the crack of dawn, I was back in my original camp below the bridge feeling very weak and nauseous.

I had walked downstream for an hour or so that morning but progress through thick, soft sand was very slow. The river itself was as magnificent as ever, even if there was no water. Elephants were everywhere and although in general, they ignored me, the countryside had an almost primordial aura about it and I felt terribly insignificant while walking along. This really was old time Africa in the raw.

I was eventually driven back to my camp by swarms of particularly vicious tsetse fly. They hit me in wave after wave of stinging insects and made progress very slow and painful until I was eventually forced to run back through the sand – not an enjoyable exercise in that heat. Tsetse fly were eradicated from this area of the Zambezi Valley many years ago but with the economic disasters affecting most government departments in Zimbabwe, tsetse control had obviously been forgotten or was regarded as unimportant.

My camp was a comfortable one and I was pleased with it. I had laid my ground sheet and sleeping mat out below a reasonably shady tree and on top of them was my blanket, covered by a 'sheet bag' – merely a double sheet, sewn up along one edge so that I could climb into it as I would a proper sleeping bag. My pack made a comfortable backrest during the day and my discarded clothing did duty as my nighttime pillow. If it hadn't been for the oppressive heat, I would have been enjoying myself.

On my way back to camp, I almost ran into an elephant cow with a tiny calf at heel. She shook her head and mock charged through the sand while junior squealed, but she wasn't serious so I stood my ground and she turned off with a shrill scream of disgust. Such wonderful animals, elephant. I much prefer them to my own species.

My problem was what to do for the rest of the day that wouldn't make me more fretful and anxious. This was my sort of countryside but it was far too hot to explore my surroundings. All I could do was sit around in what sparse shade I could find and think about what I was going to do next.

I could either have another try at getting down the river or I could keep on the road until I reached Gache Gache – the next major river on my route. The main problem with the latter choice was that I had no idea how far I would have to walk or whether there was any water along the way.

My body felt as though I had been hit by a truck and that did nothing to ease my mind. If I felt this bad after a few days on the road, how was I going to survive the next few weeks?

I forced down two meals that morning in an effort to build up some strength. The meals in a mug were not inspiring but for the moment, I had water from the spring and I knew I had to get some sort of sustenance down me.

Filling up my water bags early that morning, I had found that one was leaking from the cap. No matter how I tightened it – and I didn't dare be too rough – precious liquid seeped from beneath the plastic screw top. It was another worry but I carefully packed both plastic bags in the side pockets of my pack so that provided I kept the pack upright, I shouldn't lose too much water. What a disappointment those water bags were turning out to be. I had tested them exhaustively back in England and they had held up well under all sorts of punishment. Made by Cascade Designs in Seattle, the manufacturers' blurb built them up as indestructible. I couldn't help wondering how much worse I would have felt if I was walking in the desert.

Another problem with kit and equipment was the fact that my dictaphone had died on me. I tried my best to repair it but couldn't see the trouble and had no wish to carry any extra weight, so wrapping it together with a dozen spare tapes securely in a plastic bag, I dropped the little parcel deep into the bole of a big mopani tree. It should be there still so perhaps one day I will go back and retrieve it. For the duration of my walk however, I would have to rely on my own handwriting – illegible at the best of times. I would also miss the sound of a human voice, even if it was only my own.

As the sun went down on my second day in the Nyaodza, the flies and insects disappeared apart from occasional stragglers. Hot, sweaty but vaguely content, I sat in my sheet bag, lit my pipe and waited for night to fall. The stars were out in full force and I could hear a bushbuck barking in the hills. It was a lovely evening and for a brief moment, I was completely at peace. It was the sort of moment that if I finished the walk, would lighten my memories for years to come, even when the hardships of the trip had been long forgotten. Had I not been so worried about the weeks ahead of me, I would have been really enjoying myself.

❧

Before I started my walk to Binga, I had set my sights on covering about fifteen kilometres a day, but on my sixth day out from Kariba, I did over thirty-five kays and ended up in exactly the same place as I had started. It was not one of the better ones.

Having made my decision during the evening, I hit the road for Gache Gache at first light and covered seventeen kilometres in the first three hours.

I saw a number of buffalo, kudu and waterbuck along the way. A warthog family startled me by jumping out of the grass almost beneath my feet, but any joys I might have felt at being in wild Africa were quickly dissipated by repeated attacks from tsetse and biting flies. Did I really do this for fun I wondered or did I get some sort of perversely masochistic thrill out of suffering? The questions were unanswerable. To add to my problems, my right knee was very sore and the stitching was tearing loose on one shoulder strap of my pack. I couldn't help wondering whether I was in better condition than my kit or the other way around. The sole of my boot was definitely coming away – I hadn't thought to bring a tube of glue - and although I could probably stitch up the pack strap, I felt it ought to be done by an expert.

At one stage during the first couple of hours, I heard a vehicle and might easily have accepted a lift but perhaps fortunately, it was going in the other direction. It contained four white men and the driver waved briefly, the passenger looked thunderstruck and the two in the back slept. Amazed at seeing an elderly white man alone – and walking – out here perhaps, but they didn't stop to ask what or how I was doing. If any of them ever read this narrative, thanks for your concern Fellows

Once again, I couldn't eat because water was short, but I made a small camp in a dry riverbed and tried to wait out the heat of the day. It was not easy. Mopani bees buzzed irritatingly around my face, probing into my ears, eyes and mouth in their eternal quest for moisture. Although they are completely harmless, they arrive in such vast numbers and are so difficult to get rid of that they can drive the strongest of men or women to drink. At one stage, I donned my face veil, which at least made them keep their distance, but was claustrophobically stifling. By midday, I was desperate for a snooze, but couldn't find a patch of shade large enough to lie down in. There were no leaves on the riverside trees and the surrounding countryside was so desolate that the only signs of life were the mopani bees, the flies and the occasional foraging ant. There weren't even any birds to be

seen or heard and that is a rare occurrence in the
Zambezi Valley. I wrote about my feelings of despair in
my journal.

*'Wondering to myself whether I experienced similarly
lousy days when cycling or rowing. I must have done in
Hobo but at least I wasn't thirsty. I know I had some
pretty bleak days on my bike too, but I could always
move on when my spirits were low. I am in a weird sort
of vicious circle here. The hotter and more bored I
become, the more I drink and the more danger I put
myself into. I can't move on either or the sun will literally kill me. Why do I do this to myself?'*

It was an unanswerable question but by mid afternoon, I was in a mess. My water was hot and did little to
assuage my thirst, with the result that craving relief I
drank more, even though I knew it was daft. My lips
were blistered from the sun and my limbs felt drained of
strength. Once again I was faced with a difficult choice.

I would have to walk again as soon as the temperature
dropped but which way should I go. I had no idea how
far I was from Gache Gache so although the road offered
fairly easy walking, it could prove to be a death trap if I
couldn't find water. Walking directly west toward the lake
was another option but once again, I had no idea how far
I was from the shoreline and if the going was rough as it
seemed likely to be, I would use up even more water.

The third alternative was to retrace my steps and
return to my little spring under the Nyaodza bridge. I
didn't want to go backwards and I had already spent two
whole days beneath that bridge, but at least I knew there
was plenty of water there and it would give me a chance
to ease out the kinks in my body and thoroughly think
out my plans.

The fact that if I didn't reach a water source within twenty-four hours I would die, also provided serious motivation for heading in the one direction, I knew there was a spring.

It wasn't really much of a choice so as the sun started to fall, I wearily hauled my pack on to my back once more and set off toward my little spring. It was a decision that was to affect the entire course of my walk.

CHAPTER TWO

(Under Arrest)

I should have been enjoying myself. It was a lovely evening, I was walking along a remote road in wild Africa and although I was heading in the wrong direction, at least I was walking toward water.

Deep in my heart, perhaps I was enjoying the walk. I certainly appreciated the harsh beauty of my surroundings and there was plenty of wild life around me now that I had left the horrors of my little riverbed. A young kudu bull watched me warily from a copse of tall trees and guinea fowl cackled mockingly as they scurried across the road. At one point, I stopped to check the cause of a tree moving about and the elephant bull looked vaguely surprised when he saw me. This was what I had dreamed about in England and it was only the fact that I was tired, sore, thirsty and going in the wrong direction that dragged my spirits down.

It must have been around six in the evening when I saw a vehicle coming toward me. I stopped politely on the side of the road and waited for them to pass, but they wheeled to a dusty halt beside me. The vehicle was an open safari truck that had once belonged to the United Touring Company and I studied the occupants with interest.

There were two black hunters in the front and their clients, who looked vaguely Eastern European perched comfortably on the high raised seat in the rear. All four were carrying heavy rifles and if they were surprised to see me, nobody mentioned it.

"What are you doing in our concession?" demanded the hunter in the front passenger seat. His tone was angrily contemptuous and I felt myself bristling. Inwardly advising myself to stay cool, I answered politely.

"I am walking to Binga, but ran out of water so am heading back to the Nyaodza."

"This is our hunting concession and you are not allowed here." He brushed my explanation aside.

"I am on a public road which happens to pass through your concession. Anyone is entitled to use the road. On the other hand, if you want to take me on to Gache Gache and out of your concession, that would be a great help?"

He was not to be wheedled.

"We are busy. We do not have time to get stupid white men out of trouble. You will be eaten by lions or perhaps..." for the first time, he looked vaguely amused... "there will be a shooting accident if we happen to see you in our concession again."

"Thanks for your help." I said shortly and trying to look as disdainful as I could, hitched the pack more comfortably on to my back and walked on toward the Nyaodza. I could feel four pairs of eyes focussed on the centre of my spine for a minute or so, then the truck started up and roared away toward Gache Gache. I had a feeling I would hear more of that unpleasant little encounter and I wasn't wrong.

One of my reasons for starting the walk toward the end of October was that it is also the end of the official hunting season. As I walked back toward Nyaodza, I couldn't help wondering if anyone still took any notice of that in modern Zimbabwe. That little party had obviously been intent on shooting something so it certainly didn't seem like it. I wondered how much trouble they were going to cause me and whether I should forsake the road, take to the bush and follow elephant roads along the lakeshore. I did not want to end up with a bullet in me but there was still the problem of water.

My meeting with the hunters had ruined any enjoyment I might have been feeling about my surroundings and it took me another four hours to plod back to the river. Hills that hadn't seemed particularly steep that morning, now loomed like towering mountains and my legs began to feel rubbery with effort and lack of sustenance. I hadn't eaten since first light and although I wasn't hungry, I knew I had to get something into my system. All I had was a small packet of tiny fruit flakes. They were hardly substantial, but they were sweet and tasted absolutely divine. Suddenly I wished I had brought more of them but I only had about twenty-five packets in my pack so they would need to be rationed very carefully.

It was dark long before I reached the Nyaodza, but I was too fed up with life to care. With only a couple of kilometres to go, I heard a vehicle coming up behind me and threw myself into the long grass beside the road. I didn't know why I was hiding, but I don't think I was overly surprised to see my unfriendly hunting party moving slowly along while shining a big spotlight into the bush on both sides of the road. Whether they were looking for me or not, I had no way of knowing but I let them go and didn't move again until the noise of the engine had entirely disappeared.

Feeling weary and somewhat fretful, I finally curled up in a hurriedly laid bed beside the familiar spring. I had covered close to forty kilometres and was right back where I started.

At nine the next morning, I was sitting in the shade of the bridge, my body aching abominably and my feet submerged in the spring. They were very sore and blistered, probably because I had taken my shoes off during the previous afternoon and burnt the soles of my feet on the hot sand. It seemed the perfect excuse to rest up another day, do my laundry and an inventory of kit damage. It is often said that there is no hurry in Africa and I had shade and water – two infinitely precious commodities. Doing nothing in the sun on one of the continent's most spectacular rivers seemed infinitely preferable to another day of long, hot, thirsty walking.

It seemed strange when I was so hot but I had woken in the early hours with my teeth chattering from the cold. It was a beautiful clear night, but I had to use the blanket I had seriously thought about leaving behind to save on weight. I could only assume the cold was some sort of reaction to a hellish day in the sun when I doubtless sweated off a great deal of body fat.

Although that day passed slowly, it was not at all boring. I heard elephant throughout the morning, a couple of old buffalo bulls wandered by at lunchtime and while I was again soaking my feet prior to an afternoon siesta, two young bushbuck came down to drink from my spring. The heat was obviously getting to them too as they ignored me and drank hugely, less than three metres from where I sat. For such shy creatures, that was either boldness or desperation to a marked degree. I promptly named the spring 'Bushbuck Pool.'

At one stage during that fiendishly hot afternoon, I was trying to work out how much water I had drunk during my week on the road. It had to be well over sixty litres. Me, who in normal times, doesn't drink water at all unless it is flavoured with a goodly dollop of whisky.

Just after first light the next morning, they came for me. I was filling my water bags from the spring, when I heard the rumble of a vehicle approaching and when it came to a halt on the bridge above me, stuck my head out to have a look.

There must have been a dozen of them, all armed and all crammed into a battered looking land rover bearing the insignia of the National Parks department.

"Good morning Gentlemen," I said politely and the driver swung himself out of the cab and peered down at me.

"What are you doing?" He asked mildly and encouraged by his lack of hostility, I explained that I was walking to Binga.

"Ah," he said as if that explained a great deal. "My name is Newton. I have things to check but we will be back here in thirty minutes to sort out this mess. Don't leave here please."

"Of course I won't," Had a helpful vehicle come along, I would most certainly have boarded it and got myself as far away as possible but I wasn't telling him that. As soon as the truck was out of sight, I packed up my gear, hid my thunder flashes under the bridge and waited with as much nonchalance as I could muster to be arrested.

I guessed what must have happened. The hunting party I had met the other night would have radioed through to Parks and told them to get rid of me. Newton had gone on to check the story with them and would then have to get me out of the area. I knew there was a hunting camp somewhere up ahead belonging to Vice President Joice Mujuru and as my hostile friends had been driving a government-sponsored truck, I had no doubt at all that they were part of her set up. Parks would have no option but to take me back to Kariba.

While I was waiting for the return of Newton and his merry men, I heard another vehicle approaching from the Kariba direction. I climbed up on to the road, prepared to wave them down and ask for a lift out of the immediate area. That would sort the hunters out, I thought. It wasn't to be, as the vehicle that appeared was the UTC truck with the same four aboard.

"What are you doing?" The passenger was again the spokesman and he shouted the question at me.

"Walking to Binga," I was deliberately obtuse. "I told you the other evening."

He smiled somewhat smugly.

"I have told you what will happen if we catch you in our concession," he said. "I think I will call up the army when I get back to camp and have you taken away. They will sort you out."

I had no doubt that they would.

"Call up who you like," I muttered wearily and waved him away.

It was only when they had gone that I realised that neither the driver nor the clients had said a single word throughout our two meetings.

I had been carrying a cell phone in my pack, even though there was no reception around the lakeshore. My intention had been to announce my arrival at Binga to my nearest and dearest and in order to preserve battery life (my wind-up charger was hard work) I carried the phone separated into component parts. This seemed an opportune moment to assemble it again so I did and slipped it into a pocket. It could prove helpful if the situation became nasty.

Newton's thirty minutes became an hour and then two hours but eventually they trundled into sight again. He came over to where I was sitting on a rock.

"Can I see your permit?" He asked and I shook my head.

"I don't need a permit to walk along the road. It is a public highway."

"This is Charara hunting area so you need a permit." He was still polite.

"Would I need a permit if I was driving along this road?"

"No." He shook his head.

"Would I need a permit if I was cycling along this road."

"No," His eyes narrowed as he realised where I was going.

"Then why should I need a permit when I am walking along this road?"

"This is parks land so you need a permit."

I felt a little sorry for Newton. He was young and in charge but I don't think he was entirely sure what to do about an elderly white man doing something he must have considered foolhardy and totally without reason.

"Get in the truck," he said tersely. "We can sort the matter out in Kariba."

"Listen Newton," I was aghast at the prospect of going back even though I knew it was inevitable. "I have walked all the way from Kariba and it has taken me a week. Are you going to bring me back here when the matter is sorted out?"

He smiled and didn't answer, merely gesturing me toward the land rover. Wearily throwing my pack into the back, I climbed in among the others and sat wedged uncomfortably in one corner while they plied me with questions.

"Why are you doing this *Madhala*?" The Chishona word means 'old man' and it felt very apt. I shrugged my reply.

"I just want to walk to Binga."

"What about lions? There are many in this area. Aren't you scared of being eaten?"

Looking for a reaction, I showed them the two weirdly shaped rocks hung around my neck. They were encapsulated in black cord and had been given to me by self-proclaimed white witch, Di Wright to protect me from the 'undead.' I wore them to humour her but suddenly I was very glad I had.

"Those are my '*mashonga*,'" (amulet) I told the questioner. "They protect me from wild animals and from stupid people who work for National Parks."

The questions stopped but I listened with interest to them arguing among themselves. They were all tough, brash young men, proud of their uniforms and their rifles, but like most Africans, wary of the authority of age. In my case, the age was compounded by eccentricity, which they couldn't understand and they argued long and hard about what ought to be done with me. One or two felt I should be handed over to the police or army, but the majority seemed to feel that I should either be let off with a fine or left to get on with my walk.

In the meantime, those long kilometres that had taken me nearly a week of painful progress to cover, unrolled steadily behind me. I watched them go with a sick feeling in my tummy.

The parks men were still arguing when we got to Nyanyana, a small sub office some ten kilometres outside Kariba. I breathed a sigh of relief that they hadn't taken me right into town. Seizing the opportunity, I sent a quick text to Geoff Blyth, advising him what had happened and asking him to keep an eye on the situation. I didn't want to disappear into a police cell without anyone knowing where I was.

In the main office, the discussions went on and as is often the way in Africa, voices were raised and the decibels mounted with ever increasing excitement. I was obviously a spy. I should be handed over to the army, to Special Branch or the CIO. I was too old to be a spy. I was obviously mad as a hatter. Look at how thin I was. I would never get to Binga so it was surely better to let me go on and die in the bush. My Chishona isn't perfect but I could follow the arguments although I tried to look as though I didn't have a clue what they were talking about.

The squabble was brought to a stop by the arrival of a thin young woman in civilian clothing who told everybody to be quiet. Newton stood attentively beside her. Once the hubbub had died down, she turned to me.

"What are you doing Mr Lemon?" She asked me quietly.

"I am walking to Binga Ma'am. Are you the warden?"

"I am the acting warden. Why are you walking to Binga?"

The conversation was taking its usual somewhat surreal turn and I struggled to answer the question adequately. I couldn't.

"There is no answer to that. I just want to walk to Binga around the lake shore."

She looked steadily at me and I could see reluctance in her eyes. Hope flared in my breast.

"I shall have to fine you, you know. Even if you were on a road, when my patrol found you, you were getting water from the riverbed. You need a permit for that."

"Semantics, Ma'am. How much do I have to pay?"

A fine would suit me down to the ground. I didn't want to be handed over to other departments for further interrogation and was anxious to get out of there before anyone else came along.

Acting Warden Alice Samakane frowned and slipped a book out from under the desk. She riffled the pages briefly, but I had the feeling she was only going through the motions.

"One thousand dollars," there was a small smile in her eyes and I restrained myself from grinning delightedly. At the black market exchange rate of the time, that amounted to a princely fifty pence and even I could afford that. I could have hugged the lass. That would have given her a shock as quite apart from her official dignity, I don't suppose I was at my most pre-possessing.

The men around me, obviously disappointed that the fun was over began to disperse and I counted out the money while the acting warden made out a receipt. There was another moment of angst when she asked for my identification. All I had was my son Brian's metal ID card and I hesitantly handed it across the desk. Brian was

born on the same day as me but the years were obviously very different. This was spotted by a sharp-eyed game scout, looking over my shoulder.

"How could you have been born in 1965?" he demanded and Ms Simakane looked briefly interested.

"It was one of those silly mistakes when the card was issued," I blustered. "They read it as 65 instead of 45 from the form and so I am stuck with it. If I hand it in to be changed, it could take two or three years to get it back. You know what those people are like."

The acting warden grunted an agreement and the scout withdrew somewhat reluctantly. I don't think he believed me and I can only apologise to him now for my blatant lie.

"What are you going to do now?" Ms Samakane handed me the receipt.

"I will get someone to take me out again and continue my walk."

She shook her head in mock sorrow but didn't ask any more questions.

"Just don't offend anyone else." She said mildly and I left the building, thankful for the abundant common sense of Acting Warden Alice Samakane. What a splendid lady she proved to be.

Another splendid lady was waiting for me in the camp outside. On receipt of my text, Geoff had sent his wife Nikki to keep an eye on things and I was overjoyed to see her, particularly as she presented me with an ice cold coca cola. The poor girl was subjected to a prickly kiss and a somewhat smelly hug before we drove quickly away from the camp in case the acting warden changed her mind.

"We have all been so worried about you," Nikki told me. "The temperature over the past week has been in the middle forties and nobody thought you could possibly survive."

I wanted to cry. Somebody cared and the hardships of the previous week would soon be forgotten.

"What are you going to do now?" Nikki glanced across at me.

"Get someone to drive me back out and carry on." I told her briefly. "I am not going to be beaten by ruddy National Parks or the hunting fraternity."

She smiled and I knew I had said the right thing.

"I'm sure Geoff will take you out but you must rest for a couple of days first. You have lost a lot of weight."

When I examined my fine receipt later that day, my name was given as Mr Lemon and the ID card details were Brian's so my eldest son now has a conviction in Zimbabwe for entering Parks and Wild Life land without a permit. Truly life in Africa can be strange.

CHAPTER THREE

(The Road to Sanyati)

There is something about sleeping under a big baobab tree that soothes the soul – mine at any rate. After two days of pure relaxation with the Blyths, during which I ate, drank (even a few beers) and generally relaxed, Geoff drove me to a point close to that horrible little river bed where I had spent a hellish day and I left the road and headed for the mouth of the Gache Gache river.

Rested and refreshed with plenty of water in my containers, I made good progress before stumbling across what looked like a well-used road heading in the right direction. I followed this and came to the picturesque Gache Gache lodge, where manager Stan Newman made me very welcome. It was lovely. At Stan's invitation I stayed the night and ate and drank some more, before being shown off in the right direction the next morning. I was heading for Nyamhunga fishing village and then the Sanyati Gorge, but somehow managed to bypass the fishing village altogether. I eventually found a huge baobab close to the shore where I set up my camp.

Judging by the girth of its trunk, the tree had to be at least eight hundred years old. I was unlikely to be the first person to use it as a temporary home, but it stirred my ever-vivid imagination. What stories these trees could tell if only they could speak.

Sitting by my fire that evening, I couldn't help reflecting that in a weird sort of way, those hunters had done me a huge favour and probably rescued my trip from being a total failure. Thanks to the wisdom and kindness of Alice Samakane, I was now rested, refreshed and mentally far more able to cope with whatever lay ahead. I had talked things through with Geoff and Nikki, discarded my spicier meals which would only add to my thirst and even attended six year old Bronwen's birthday party, where my bristly chin was a hit with all the little ones. With Gache Gache behind me and my sore feet feeling considerably better, I felt fit enough and strong enough to make the Sanyati Gorge, another forty odd kilometres ahead. I had also turned right around the end of the lake and was at last walking in the right direction.

Sanyati would pose another huge problem, but I was determined not to worry about it until I had to make decisions. A far cry indeed from my fretful anxiety of that first terrible week, when every minor problem assumed major significance and my mind was in an absolute mess. In the modern world, we often complain about feeling thirsty, but nobody who has not endured real thirst and the fear it engenders can understand just how it affects the mind. I had been lucky and determined to stay as close as possible to the lake shore for the rest of the trip. If that meant walking a few extra kilometres, that was too bad. I was not going to be thirsty again.

The heat was still appalling and I could almost feel the weight dropping off me but I was learning to cope with it. I would rise at four thirty, brew tea or coffee on a fire, and then start walking at five. This gave me three hours of relatively easy going and I tried to push myself on and cover as much distance as I could in those hours. At eight or thereabouts, I would stop, rest, enjoy the scenery and smoke a gently soothing pipe. If there was a nice spot for a day camp in view, I would make myself a meal and then sit out the hot hours when the sun was like a hammering furnace in the sky. If there was nowhere suitable for the purpose, I would move on, but at a more leisurely pace until I found a nice spot. The difficulty was always shade. This was mopani country and mopani trees have few leaves until the rains arrive. It was often a case of finding a tree with a very thick trunk and moving around it as the sun shifted across the sky.

Although I tried always to keep the lake in view and tended to panic a little when it wasn't, the water level was so low that refilling my containers often necessitated a long walk through reeds or swampy ground. I wore a handkerchief around my forehead to keep sweat out of my eyes and another one around my neck to keep me cool. Whenever I could, I doused these in water, but such was the heat that they would be dry again within minutes. The only thing that remained wet was my shirt, but that was drenched in sweat and by the end of the day was often quite unpleasant.

The days were long but they were relatively peaceful and those few Tonga I met along the way were usually too polite to query my reasons for walking along this wild shoreline with a huge blue pack on my back. One or two walked with me for a while and we exchanged desultory conversation about my destination, the state of the fishing industry and the world in general. For any Tonga, the two main centres of world civilisation are Kariba and Binga, so apart from the fact that the two little towns were a long way apart, most of these friendly men and women thought it perfectly reasonable that I was exchanging the comforts of one for the comforts of the other. The only thing they were not able to fathom was why I didn't make the journey by bus.

At one stage on my way to water, I inadvertently dropped the pedometer fitted to my belt. I hadn't noticed the loss but on my way back from the lake, a young man called Meeting was waiting for me. He gravely handed the instrument over and I then had to explain what it was – not an easy matter when one party to the conversation has only a few words of English and the other has precisely three words of Chitonga.

We managed though and when he heard that I was walking to Binga, Meeting was truly impressed. Having tried the weight of my pack on his shoulders, he shook his head in bemusement, but instead of thinking me crazy, he solemnly told me, "You are a man among men, Good Sir."

It was great for the ego but I wished he had offered to carry that damned pack a little way for me. It was a funny thing about that pack. When I was rowing the lake, I formed a huge and intimate bond with my trusty dinghy. When I was cycling down Africa, I almost fell in love with my garish yellow bicycle, but I never could develop any sort of rapport with my backpack. As time went on, it seemed to become heavier rather than lighter and eventually, I hated it with sincere passion. It was quite a nice pack too and had probably cost more than either my dinghy or my bicycle.

One morning I found a large fig tree almost within sight of the water. It cast abundant shade and although it was close to a village, the opportunity to escape the heat for a while was too good to miss. I crawled into that lovely, lovely shade, spread my ground sheet and drifted off to sleep.

When I awoke some time later, I was surrounded by goats. This was the wild Zambezi Valley, filled with lions, leopards, buffalo and all sorts of dangerous animals yet I was in the middle of a herd of ordinary domestic goats – *mbudzi* to the Shona. It surely couldn't be good for tourism.

It was immediately obvious that I was lying under the goats' tree and they stood watching me, patiently waiting for me to move. When at last it became obvious that I had no intention of doing so, individual animals sidled closer and eventually one large billy goat flopped down onto his knees less than two metres from me. With a disgusted grunt, he lay down, farted noisily and went to sleep. Moments later, the others had followed suit and I looked hungrily at them. It was a long time since I had seen so much meat, even if it was still on the hoof.

My own chances of sleep had obviously come to an end, so I busied myself with a meal, tea and a general sorting out of my kit. The nearest goat, opened one eye, looked and then went back to sleep. I was dirty and probably smelled bad but the water was a goodly distance away so I decided that a bath could wait.

I had almost finished my meal when six children emerged from the nearby bushes. They were dressed in rags and probably smelled pretty bad themselves, but they were totally intrigued by my presence so close to their homes. Sitting in the dust three metres in front of me, they examined me intently and in complete silence. I gazed back and the goats, sensing the possibility of disturbance, languidly rose to their feet, dusted themselves off and drifted away among the trees. I was left with my audience of *picannins*.

"Hello," I ventured but six blank stares greeted the words.

"*Mavuka biyeni*," I had learned how to say it in Chitonga before leaving Kariba, but not an eye flickered or a muscle moved. They just stared.

I tried ignoring them completely and read a bit of Oscar Wilde, but every time I looked up from the Great Man's words, six pairs of eyes were still fixed unwaveringly upon me. I was beginning to feel distinctly uncomfortable.

Eventually my frayed nerves exploded into temper.

"Go on, bugger off," I shouted, gesturing with my hands so that they could have no doubt what I meant. "This is my camp and I don't want you here."

Rising to my feet, I picked up a twig from the ground nearby and gestured threateningly in their direction. Not a muscle moved and I wondered what to do.

"Oh hell! Go away," I yelled and this time I ran in their direction. Moving with incredible speed and agility, they were on their feet and had almost disappeared before I took my second step. For an hour or so afterwards, I heard the occasional whispered comment and isolated giggle so they hadn't gone far but at least I no longer had to feel like some exotic specimen in the zoo.

It was late afternoon, my remaining water was hot and I was debating the wisdom of a walk in the sun to get more when my next unannounced visitor arrived. A short, thickset young man he introduced himself as Happymore Chaminuka and cheerfully informed me that he was 'possessed by the Spirits.'

Instinctively, I felt for the stones around my neck. Could this be one of Di Wright's mysterious 'undead?' But no, Happymore was a friendly young man and wanted nothing more than a bit of conversation. His command of English was excellent and this was a chance for him to practise.

"I am a very fine singer," he told me seriously. "I can also act very well so although I am an itinerant preacher at the moment, I intend to take up a career on the stage."

Having learned that he was thirty four, I told him that he had better hurry with that particular career option, as both acting and singing were best embarked upon at a much younger age that that.

"I shall be alright," Happymore was obviously confident. "I am very talented you know. I can speak seven languages including Afrikaans."

Happymore went on to tell me all about the life and times of Happymore for a while and seeking to get rid of him, I told him that I needed to fill my water containers so would be going down to the lake.

"I shall accompany you," was his response so off we went together. It was another of those lovely Kariba bays with abundant bird life and two hippo chortling near the mouth, but I had little opportunity to savour it as my companion chattered incessantly. It was when we were on our way back to the fig tree that he brought me to a sudden halt.

"I think I will walk with you to Binga," Happymore sounded thoughtful. "You will need company and I am an excellent cook."

Was there nothing that this paragon couldn't do? However, he was NOT walking with me or he would drive me mad with his chatter. I didn't want to offend him though so I remained polite.

"You had better not Happymore," I told him mildly. "You would not be able to keep up with me," – a blatant lie as at that stage a heavily pregnant tortoise could have outpaced me – "and besides, I am not very good company when I travel."

To prove my point, I showed him a photograph I had taken of myself when I was worrying about water at the Nyaodza bridge. It was pretty horrific. My chin was stubbled, my lips were puffed up with blisters and my expression was bleak in the extreme. I think it put him off because he didn't mention the matter again.

On our return to the fig tree, I was horrified to see that the six *picannins* had been replaced by all their families. There were no adult men present, but the clearing was full of women of all ages, children and a few teenagers of both sexes. They stood in a wide semi circle, gazing with interest at my bedroll and the pack, propped against the tree. There was a hum of conversation and I looked a little nervously at my companion.

"What do they want, Happymore?" I tried to sound more confident than I felt. "Tell them to go away."

Happymore laughed.

"They have come to see you," he told me. "The only white people they have ever seen before are hunters who drive past in their trucks. These people weren't sure that *'warungu'* (white people) had legs and the children told them that you have a normal body so they have come to check."

It was back to being an exhibit for a while although this time it wasn't in silence. The villagers chattered cheerfully among themselves and I didn't think I wanted

49

to know what they were saying. Two youngsters were walking around the clearing collecting large sticks and bits of wood, which they placed beside the tiny twigs I had assembled for my evening fire. I have never made large fires in the bush and I asked Happymore what they were up to.

"They say that your fire will be too small. There are lots of buffalo in this area and they want you to be safe."

"Tell them I will be fine," I scoffed to hide my appreciation of such concern for my welfare. "I am quite accustomed to buffalo.

'Please also tell them," I tried to sound firm, "that it was lovely to meet them all but could everyone now leave me alone as I have much communing to do with my own spirits."

The assembled gathering obviously understood this and with little murmurs of 'byee byee' and dainty curtseys and clapping of hands from the young women, they melted away into the evening. Shortly afterwards, Happymore shook my hand and made his departure, leaving me alone to reflect on a very strange day.

I stuck with my small fire that evening and went to bed feeling pretty good, but when I opened my eyes just before dawn, I found myself under intense scrutiny once again. This time, the curious one was a massively built buffalo bull, which stood less than two metres from where I lay and peered at me in evident perplexity. He was so close that I could smell him and I lay as still as I could while he sniffed aloud in his efforts to find out what I was. It was probably those sniffs that had woken me up.

Eventually the old boy gave up on me and with a sudden swinging movement of his head, wheeled around and flounced toward the gathering day. I smiled in my enjoyment of the moment and couldn't help feeling warm toward those lovely Tonga who had irritated me intensely, even though they only had my welfare at heart.

I was finishing my tea when Happymore reappeared to see me off. We parted with handshakes and promises to keep in touch, although how either of us could possibly keep to that I didn't know. I set out on what would be the last lap to Sanyati, feeling suddenly confident in my own ability to cope and pleased that if this was to be my last little adventure, it was being done among the lovely Tonga people who have been so kind to me over the years.

Mind you, I was well aware that from now on, I would have no roads to follow and many more difficulties to cope with. The only consoling prospect about the days to come was that at least I would never be far from water.

Shortly after leaving Happymore under the giant fig tree, I had another very strange encounter with buffalo. I spotted a group of the big animals inshore from me as I walked and moments later, they saw me. Wheeling as one, they trotted inquisitively toward me and I froze in my tracks, my eyes swivelling in search of suitable trees to climb should their curiosity get the better of them. There were none. I was walking through ankle high grass and the buff were between me and the nearest trees.

There was nothing I could do except stand perfectly still. I inwardly debated slipping my pack off in case I had to run, but there was nowhere to run to and it might well have proved fatal anyway so I left everything where it was. Trotting in line abreast, the buffalo stopped about twelve metres from me and yet again, I found myself under intense scrutiny. They stared, I stared back and none of us moved a muscle. I could actually feel my heart thudding against the wall of my chest, although I wasn't particularly scared. I've known many people killed by buffalo but always by a single animal – usually a wounded bull. I didn't know of any incident where a group had actually chased or harmed anyone so I waited and watched to see what they would do.

At some unseen and unheard signal, they made up their collective mind that I was harmless and swung around to trot back to where they had been when they first spotted me. I gave them a moment and then resumed my walk. At my first movement, they swung around again and back they came – a line of very black buffalo looking for all the world like a group of immense rugby forwards. The All Blacks forward pack, magnified three times perhaps.

Halting in my tracks again, I waited for them to stop but this time they seemed even more curious. The lead animals slowed, but they didn't stop and I could feel my muscles tense as the distance between us lessened rapidly. This time, they could not have been more than ten metres from me and it seemed a good deal less. I could hear the gusty sounds of their breathing and the occasional clatter as horn banged against horn. What would they do? I hardly dared breathe myself.

I don't know how long we stood staring at each other. It could have been five seconds, it could have been five minutes, it might almost have been five hours. Time seemed to stand completely still but eventually they once again decided that I posed no threat, wheeled around and ran off again, huge black bottoms swaying away through the grass.

More cautiously this time, I resumed my walk and one or two individual animals looked up to see where I was going. They were evidently satisfied that I was harmless, as there were no more approaches and I was able to get myself out of sight with an explosive sigh of relief. I like buffalo but they are awfully large and somewhat scary when standing in a threatening mass of muscle. I think I would rather face up to the All Blacks.

I was asked at Sanyati Lodge whether I was enjoying myself and in truth it was a difficult question to answer. There had been some magical moments that would live on in my memory for ever. I had covered over two hundred kilometres and met some extremely nice people. I was a hundred percent fitter than I had been on starting out and was almost managing to cope with the furnace-like heat. I should have been enjoying myself but my mind was in a turmoil with doubts and fears about the way ahead. Sanyati would provide me with my first major hurdle, as I would have to cross the great gorge and get into the Matusadona National Park where I would face a whole new set of problems.

Just crossing the gorge was an awesome challenge and had been worrying me for a while. The obvious way was to go by boat across the mouth but that meant finding someone to take me. The gorge itself cut steeply inland for about twenty kilometres before it was narrow enough to wade across and although that didn't seem a vast distance in the context of my walk,

I knew from past experience that it would be hellishly difficult going.

A series of horrifyingly steep ridges stretched inland from the mouth of the gorge. Their slopes were covered with gravel and scree, there were few handholds and the risk of a bad fall in those hills was terrifying real. I had once walked from the top of the gorge down the other side and nearly died. I was young then too, so what it would be like at my current venerable age, I didn't know and was scared to find out. Nevertheless, I had to cross the gorge. The alternative was to abort the trip, turn back and walk all the way back to Kariba – a prospect that did not bear thinking about.

In Kariba I had spoken to a Tonga safari guide called Dollar Karingiramambo who worked at Sanyati Lodge and he told me not to worry.

"Call in, have a couple of beers and we will make a plan," he told me cheerfully so into the lodge I staggered at about 10 in the morning. It was still fiendishly hot and I had walked a long way that morning but it was good to get the pack off my back, have a cold shower and relax with a bucket full of orange juice and soda. The lodge manager, a young man named Courage offered me a staff room for the night and I didn't hesitate in accepting. Later in the morning Dollar and I discussed the problems of crossing the gorge.

"I would take you myself when I take visitors on a game drive," he offered, "but that could get me into trouble with the park warden at Tashinga if you fall foul of his patrols."

That was the most comfortable option out of the way, but he later took me to meet a group of fish poachers in a bay behind the lodge. One of them – a chap called Enat

- agreed to paddle me across the gorge in his metal dinghy for a fee of four thousand Zimbabwe dollars, which worked out at a couple of pounds. We would leave at first light the following day and although I knew it could be a hazardous journey if the wind got up, I went back to the lodge feeling infinitely better.

I passed the rest of that day in comfortable idleness. Sitting with my feet in the swimming pool and a glass of lemonade and ice in my hand, I couldn't help marvelling at how much the little things in life are appreciated when one doesn't have them. Just the fact of being cool felt overwhelmingly wonderful and when I lay down on a real bed for my afternoon nap, I thought I was in Heaven.

Lunch proved a little difficult though. There was a business conference being held at the lodge and although Dollar and I sat apart from the other guests, it was a buffet meal so I had to get up and serve myself. I could feel my stomach knotting with a feeling akin to panic as I walked across the dining room. It was probably my imagination but I felt curious eyes on me, doubtless taking in my scruffy beard, my crumpled clothing and the general decrepitude of my appearance. In such luxurious surroundings I felt like a tramp in Buckingham Palace and could feel my face reddening as I hurried back to my table. This was stupid. I was supposed to be good with people but I was genuinely scared.

They were a nice bunch though and I was plied with incredulous enquiries around the bar that evening. 'Why,' was again the most frequently asked question. I didn't know and could only shrug. I wanted to do it. That was all.

While the other guests were out on a game drive with Dollar I had shared the early evening bar with a girl called

Lara and the barman, Snap. Lara wore men's pyjamas to protect her from the sun and I wondered whether I might have coped better with trousers and a long sleeved shirt. It was too late to worry about that, but how nice it was to talk with a pretty girl over a cold beer. There are times when civilisation does beat living rough in the bush.

It was a shame to leave the comforts of Sanyati Lodge but I had a walk to complete so at first light the following day, I sat somewhat gingerly in Enat's dinghy and off we went.

Tonga fishing dinghies are issued by the government and made to a uniform pattern. They are constructed of solid metal and are about three meters long and one and a half in the beam. Although they are ruggedly stable craft, they are horribly uncomfortable. The person paddling sits on the prow while passengers perch on a very high thwart that leaves them totally exposed to the water. Even the smallest of swells brings water inboard and my first glance around the boat was to check that it contained a baler. Fortunately there were two plastic containers for the purpose. With no buoyancy tanks, the boat only needed to take in a certain amount of water to sink like a stone and that prospect was distinctly unpleasant. The deepest part of the lake, Sanyati Gorge has always been famous for the size of its crocs so I didn't fancy swimming, with or without my pack.

To make matters worse, I remembered Graeme telling me how he used to open fire on poachers in the gorge when he was working in the Matusadona with National Parks. I didn't fancy being shot at either, but to get across the river rather than detour a long way inland, I was quite prepared to change sides and take a few minor risks.

It took us about two hours to cross the mouth of the gorge and the sun was well up in the sky when I stepped somewhat shakily ashore and began to walk across the Matusadona National Park. I could only wonder what lay ahead.

CHAPTER FOUR

(The Lions of Matusadona)

The Matusadona National Park covers one hundred and forty thousand hectares of wild Africa. It is home to a wide variety of wild life, including a number of black rhinoceros, dehorned and imported from other parks where they were deemed to be more at risk from poachers. The fact that they no longer possessed horns wouldn't lessen their ferocity and I knew I would have to be careful, particularly when I reached the Tashinga area where most of the rhino had their home range.

Overlooked by the brooding Matusadona (Dung in the Road) range of mountains, the park is well known for its lion population. To my own knowledge, Matusadona lions had been responsible for four incidents of man eating over the previous twenty years and although I have never been nervous about sleeping in the open, it was a sobering thought.

Park headquarters was also at Tashinga, deep in the north western corner of the park and although there was a small sub office at Changecherere close to where I landed, Dollar had advised me to avoid this if possible.

"They will keep you there for hours, perhaps days," He warned. "Those blokes won't let you walk without a rifle and it will take time for someone to come across from Tashinga."

So it seemed that I would have to sneak through the park, not only avoiding the hazards of wild life but also taking care to avoid patrols and vehicles from park headquarters.

It was nice to be back in the Matusadona though. Over the years, I had spent a lot of time in this vast, unspoiled area. As a young copper I patrolled the hills and was pleased that on this occasion, I would be walking across the flatlands. Beautiful and remote though they were, those lofty peaks made for incredibly difficult walking. Their slopes were steep, water sources were few and far between and the danger of bumping into elephant, rhinoceros, lion or buffalo on those scrubby slopes was terrifyingly acute.

Nor was I the only family member to love the Matusadona. My son Graeme conducted walking adventure safaris in the park for years and Brian had a stint as General Manager on Fothergill Island, a luxury tourist lodge just off the shoreline. I had enjoyed holidays with friends, a honeymoon dinner and many other wonderful experiences in Matusadona and as I climbed somewhat stiffly ashore from the dinghy, it felt good to be back. From now on, it was going to be adventure all the way.

There was something rather awe inspiring about being alone and on foot in a place like the Matusadona. Having crept carefully past the buildings at Changecherere and almost walked into an old bull elephant in the process, I felt a sense of supreme relief that at last I was away from people. I reckoned that it would take me at least a week to cross the park and if I met anyone during that time, they would need to be avoided.

Although it was still terribly hot and I was losing gallons of moisture in sweat, the going was relatively easy and I always had the solace of seeing that vast expanse of lake to my right. With the drop in lake level, the bays were wider than I remembered and totally devoid of shade, but whenever I went down to refill my water containers, I was amazed at the amount of wild life I could see.

Elephant, impala, warthog, hippo, waterbuck – they all watched me with evident curiosity. The pack on my back must have made me look like a gigantic tortoise and I don't suppose they associated my scent with that of normal human beings. I also saw a number of very big crocodiles, so bathing wasn't high on my priority list.

Bird life was utterly fantastic. Huge flocks of peach-faced lovebirds rocketed by on their way to water, while in the bays, swallows and swifts performed aeronautical acrobatics, millimetres above the water. Herons, cormorants, darters, kingfishers of all types and lordly fish eagles went about their business and paid me no attention whatsoever. Saddle-billed storks and spoonbills fished unconcerned in the shallows while raptors whirled lazily in the sky above me, no doubt wondering whether I might prove edible if something went wrong.

This really was what I had embarked on my crazy venture for and for the first time since leaving Kariba, I was starting to really enjoy myself. After the thirsty horrors of that first terrible week, I had developed a miserly attitude towards water and even though I could see the lake ninety percent of the time, I made many a detour just to ensure that all my containers were full.

My first day in the park was a good one in most respects. I walked well over twenty kilometres, saw lots of wild life and enjoyed myself. The downside was that the heat was still taking enormous toll of my strength and when I set up my camp that evening, my legs were rubbery and I felt weak and nauseous. I kept telling myself not to push so hard but I had an overwhelming urge to get the kilometres behind me and so I kept going long after common sense told me to rest. My journal entry reflected the ambivalence of my feelings.

'Each day seems hotter than the one before and the heat is wearing me out but I must keep going. Was filling my water bags beside an elephant teenager this afternoon. After a quick glance, he decided I was harmless and even though there were less than ten metres between us – I was too weary to move – he played with a stick in the water and ignored me. It was lovely to be so close to a wild animal – particularly an elephant.'

As the sun went down that evening, I took a mug of tea and my pipe down to the waters edge, sat on a rock and enjoyed a spectacular sunset. A jackal wandered past but after a quick glance at me, moved on without any sign of anxiety. He obviously knew where he was going and wasn't going to be distracted by my brooding presence. That twilight sojourn was to set a pattern for the rest of the trip and even after the more horrendous days, the evening communion with my wild world was always so soothing and restful. Lake Kariba is famous for its sunsets and such is their magnificence that they never failed to repair whatever damage had been done to my soul on even the worst of days.

A pair of guinea fowl wandered down to the water close to where I was sitting and I remained as still as I possibly could. Foraging happily and chinkling quietly to each other, they obviously had no inkling of my presence and it wasn't until they were almost under my feet that they saw me, leaped squawking high in the air and ran off as fast as their little legs would take them. From a safe distance, they scolded me furiously and I smiled in satisfaction at the moment.

Listening to the news on BBC World service that evening, I learned that Saddam Hussein had been sentenced to death by a Baghdad court. It seemed strange to think that the world still went on out there. Normal lives were being led, wars were being fought and traffic was snarling up on British motorways. Lace and my family in England would be doing their Christmas shopping and decorating their houses with tinsel and holly branches while I had absolutely nothing to do. My own home was already decorated with the raw magnificence of the African bush and I needed no more. Looking straight out across the lake, I could see the lights of Kariba town twinkling distantly through the darkness. Even though those lights were a glimpse of civilisation, I was in my own wild world, sharing it with all manner of untamed animals and enjoying it immensely in my own masochistic way.

Somehow the situation seemed a little unreal, but lying on my back watching an incredible array of stars above me, I decided that I was far better off than most people – certainly better off than Mr Hussein.

A satellite twinkled its way across the velvety heavens and some of the stars seemed so close that I could almost have plucked them out of the sky. This was what my trip was all about. My first day in the Matusadona had definitely been a good one.

～

Sitting high on the remains of an abandoned houseboat that must once have been somebody's pride and joy, I reflected somewhat sourly that my first night in the park certainly had not been as enjoyable as the day it had succeeded. Appropriately in the circumstances, the houseboat had been named 'Baghdad' and I smiled when I saw the name board, but that was the only time I felt like smiling on what had already been a bad morning.

My troubles had started with the wind just before ten the previous evening. It was not just wind – it was a howling gale that descended upon my little camp like a shrieking demon. Wakened from a deep sleep by the noise, I grabbed for loose utensils and clothing that were rolling about and then curled myself into a ball and lay as still as possible, clutching my wildly flapping sheet around me. The remains of my evening fire flared and crackled, sparks flying off into the night and making me wonder if I wasn't going to start a major bush fire that would bring park patrols out in force.

There was nothing I could do about it however so I waited the storm out, feeling thankful that at least it was only wind and not rain as well. I had been praying for rain during the day but I did not want it at night. I have slept with wet clothing in wet bedding before, but it is not an experience to be recommended.

Almost as suddenly as it had started, the wind died away. It was almost as though someone had flicked a switch and silenced the weather. Breathing a sigh of relief, I sat up in my bed, still hugging the sheet to me and it was then that I heard the lions.

Deep, coughing roars seemed to reverberate around me and I decided that they could not be very far away. Such is the nature of sound in the bush that I wasn't even sure which direction the noises were coming from, but I suddenly felt awfully vulnerable. I had been more than a bit blasé about my *mashonga* with the scouts who had taken me back to Kariba, but it really did seem like a load of tripe now.

Climbing out of bed, I stoked up the fire and put a couple of larger logs on to burn. Mopani wood is wonderful stuff. It burns for ages and gives off a lovely soft fragrance, but at that stage, my nerves were a little too stretched to enjoy it. Rummaging in my pack, I brought out the thunder flashes that John Falkenberg had given me. Nothing but large and noisy firecrackers, they have a long fuse to be lit before they are thrown at whatever needs to be scared off.

Examining the damned things by torchlight, I reflected that by the time I had struck a match, lit the fuse and thrown it, any self respecting lion would have eaten me up and been waiting for his pudding and a post prandial cigar. Feeling that it was better than nothing, I laid one thunder flash, together with matches – and a lighter in case they were too damp to strike - beside my bed, adding my bush knife to the rescue package just in case things didn't go as planned. Quite how I was to fight a lion off with a small sheath knife, I wasn't sure but it had to be a comfort – I think.

The roaring gradually started to die down and I decided that the lions weren't interested in me and were moving away. In spite of the fact that my nerves were still stretched taut and twanging like guitar strings, I drifted back to sleep, only to be woken again by fat drops of rain splattering against my face.

Leaping out of bed yet again, I hurriedly climbed into my clothes, rolled up my bedding, slipped the water-proof cover over my pack and donned my poncho. Once all that was done, I sat on the pack like a mother hen, scooping anything loose such as torch, radio, camera etc under the spread of the poncho. Feeling faintly ridiculous, I waited out the storm.

Fortunately it didn't last long and half an hour later, I was back in my bed and sound asleep, but when the lions woke me with a resounding dawn chorus that seemed to literally shake the air around me, I felt gummy-eyed and irritable. When I started walking my legs felt heavy and I was decidedly out of sorts.

It was about eight in the morning when I found Bagh-dad. She rested forlornly on a knoll, her pontoons intact, but her superstructure stripped of anything valuable, including the decking planks. She must have been almost a kilometre from the water and I wondered how on earth such a large boat – she was a good fifteen metres long – had come to be abandoned in this remote spot. Smiling at the aptness of the name only a day after Saddam's sentencing, I moved reluctantly on, my eyes searching ground and bush for any sign of the lions that had so interrupted my sleep.

It looked like being another long, hard day.

The rain didn't return but the lions did. Whether they were the same lot who had disturbed my sleep that first night or not, I have no way of knowing but during my time in the Matusadona, I don't think I was ever very far from the big cats. Wherever I went, saucer-sized pug marks reminded me that danger was ever present and I walked somewhat nervously around any thicker bush I came up against, often stopping to study a thicket before venturing at all close to it and sometimes doing wide detours just in case.

One evening I was sitting on my rock enjoying the sunset when a movement to one side caught my attention. Slowly turning my head, I watched three big lionesses walking regally down to the water. They must have known I was there but they paid me no attention whatsoever. There was nothing I could do but sit still and admire the way, heavy muscles moved beneath those tawny yellow hides. I could hear them lapping noisily at the water and ten minutes later they returned, completely ignoring my presence. It was a wonderful moment in spite of my nervousness.

I don't know whether it was the same three animals or not, but later that evening when I was lying in bed admiring the night sky, lions started sounding off behind my camp. Sound travels a long way at night but this lot were undoubtedly very close and they seemed to be talking to each other rather than announcing their presence to the world, as is usual with lions. Instead of their normal throaty roars, this lot made a series of soft, grunting sounds that for some reason I found more nerve wracking than the roars would have been. It was almost as if they were debating something and I couldn't help feeling that I was the subject under discussion.

The noise went on for well over an hour and there was nothing I could do about it. At one stage, I climbed out of bed, put another log on the fire and walked around, bush knife in hand while I peered into the darkness. It was a futile exercise. Although the moon was three-quarter full and bathed the world in a pale, ethereal light – the rain had long gone – this only helped to darken the shadowy places and I knew that the lions would have chosen one such shadowy place to lie up in. As I squinted unhappily out into the half darkness, the bush itself seemed black, shadowy and full of menace. Wherever the lions were, I wasn't going to see them.

They saw me though. It was undoubtedly significant that the grunting stopped when I was moving about and recommenced once I was back in bed. Those lions were watching me and I didn't get a lot of sleep that night, even when the noise had stopped.

After the initial shower that disturbed my night so drastically, the rain seemed to have disappeared, although heavy clouds still milled about, raising the humidity level during the day to an uncomfortable degree. At times it felt as though I was walking through a gigantic sauna. Sweat streamed off me and I struggled to breathe.

Thankfully reaching a grove of trees one morning, I slipped off my pack, took out my pipe, stretched and wandered out into the open. In front of me was a wide bay and I could see fishermen in a big white cruiser casting their lines on the other side. An elephant watched them without curiosity from the bank and in a nearby tree, a fish eagle screamed its challenge.

I could feel the tension ease out of my overtaxed shoulder muscles and was about to light my pipe when I heard voices inland and very close by. For a moment, I wondered what to do. Some of the more intrepid fishermen and visitors did come ashore in the park to do a bit of gentle exploring. I had done it myself on numerous occasions, but a human presence inland was far more likely to mean trouble. Feeling suddenly threatened, I dived back into the trees and sat on my pack, trying to size up the situation.

From where I sat I could no longer hear the voices and wondered whether I had imagined them. After four weeks, my senses were far too attuned to the bush to make that sort of mistake. The interlopers were far more likely to be poachers or park personnel than wandering tourists so I had to be careful. I had been out in the open and totally exposed so they must surely have seen me. Even as I sat there, they were probably creeping up on me so deciding that anything was better than waiting for trouble, I got down on my hands and knees and crawled carefully through the trees.

I don't know what I was thinking but I had some sort of half formed idea that if there were poachers close by, I might be able to befriend them and perhaps scrounge a few bits of illegal meat to fill my horribly growling belly. On the other hand, they would probably shoot me on sight and flee, but the risk seemed worth it.

Centimetre by careful centimetre, I edged my way through the trees, taking infinite care not to make a sound. I hadn't gone far when I spotted movement through the sparse undergrowth and moments later, I could see black legs less than ten metres ahead and hear voices more plainly. They were speaking in Chishona and it didn't take long for me to realise that they were an anti poaching patrol preparing for the day ahead. Feeling distinctly fearful, I eased my way back to my pack. It seemed that this time, my venture was surely over. The patrol were so very close and must find me when they started moving. When they did, they would probably be justified in shooting me as a suspected poacher but hopefully, they were more likely to take me with them and return in triumph to Tashinga where somehow I would have to talk my way out of trouble – again. Feeling very bleak and unhappy, I waited for the inevitable arrival of the patrol.

For long minutes nothing happened. I couldn't hear anything apart from the rumble of a distant boat engine and the normal bush sounds of Africa. My nervousness mounted. Anything had to be better than waiting for capture, so eventually I snivelled through the trees again to see what was going on. Branches tore at my face and arms but I hardly noticed them. The black legs had gone and rising very carefully to my feet, I saw a long line of men walking inland and away from me. Sure enough, they wore Parks uniform and most of them carried their AK rifles slung carelessly across their shoulders.

Yet again, I had been incredibly lucky. It said little for the alertness of the patrol that they hadn't spotted me when I was out in the open and totally unaware that I had company. Now they were going about their business and I could only hope they weren't coming back.

Further investigation revealed their camp and I couldn't help a tight smile when I saw the heavy thorn *boma* they had built around their sleeping places. Heavily armed or not, these blokes weren't going to risk being surprised by lions during the night. I wondered what they would say if they could see the way I slept, totally exposed and reasonably unafraid.

The embers of what must have been an enormous fire were still glowing so I retrieved my pack, wriggled into the *boma* and made coffee. There was no point in walking on for the moment as I might well bump into the patrol again and next time I surely would not be so lucky. Laying out my ground sheet, I settled down to wait out the next few hours with a book – ironically, it was called 'Ice' and was by another eccentric wanderer, Tristan Jones, the long distance ocean sailor. The contrast between the discomfort he endured in the Polar ice pack and the discomfort I was enduring in the hot Matusadona countryside seemed to tickle my somewhat warped sense of humour, although there was nothing funny about my situation.

The day passed pleasantly enough but as evening approached, I moved away from that comfortable camp and settled myself in the bush fifty metres away. If the patrol returned, I would move further away and try to move out before they awoke the next day.

They didn't return and I was walking well before first light the following morning. That in itself was perhaps a little foolhardy but I felt that it was politic to get moving as soon as was reasonably possible. I stumbled a few times on rough ground but fortunately managed to avoid bumping into anything large and possibly dangerous. The patrol had moved inland and presumably slept inland too, so I would have to keep close to the lake shore and get as much distance under my belt as I could.

I did not want to be captured and taken to Tashinga.

～❧～

It was another early morning two days later. I had seen no more signs of the anti poaching patrol and was beginning to relax. A large rhino midden caught my eye and as I examined it to see whether anything was fresh, a heavy snort from a nearby copse sent me hurriedly on my way. It is always lovely to see rhinoceros in the wild, but they are unpredictable animals and I had no wish to find myself scurrying up trees with an angry pachyderm at my heels. Besides I wasn't sure whether I could outdistance even the blindest of rhinos with that heavy pack weighing me down.

Coming out on the edge of another wide bay, my heart sank as I saw Tashinga camp spread out before me, whitewashed buildings shining in the sun. Sitting quietly in the shade of a bush, I debated my options. The day was already well advanced and with the drop in the lake level, the shoreline in front of the camp where I had hoped to walk through unseen was horribly exposed. There was no way that I could get past without being spotted from the offices and there seemed little option but to wander in, announce my presence and pay whatever was required in the way of fines and permit fees.

The problem was that I didn't think they would let me continue. I didn't know the warden but I had been told in Kariba that he was new to his post so he was likely to do everything by the book. I didn't think park regulations would allow for an elderly wanderer with a large pack on his back – particularly when that wanderer was unarmed in an area notorious for its lions.

However, there seemed little option so I started walking again, heading deep inland to get around the bay. It was a lovely morning and a bachelor herd of young impala watched my progress with evident curiosity. I don't suppose they had seen a backpacker before. The bay seemed to go on and on for ever before fragmenting into a number of narrow creeks, all of which had to be crossed. Pausing frequently to drink and top up my belt bottle, I was making good progress, although at times I had to move among the trees and sparse patches of long grass in order to avoid being seen from the buildings of Tashinga.

After nearly an hour, I was tired and as I was still moving almost due south, it suddenly occurred to me that there was a possibility of getting right around Tashinga on the inland side. It was an option I hadn't considered but the more I thought about it, the more logical it seemed. It would mean walking hard for much of the day, branching west at a suitable point and making directly for the Ume River. The river marked the western boundary of the park and was usually well used by houseboats coming out from Kariba. If I could reach it, I was sure I would have little difficulty in getting a lift across the Ume on a houseboat tender.

The prospect brought renewed strength to my flagging legs and I pushed myself relentlessly onward. At times, it meant walking through thick bush instead of the gently open countryside I had enjoyed over the previous week but the discomfort seemed worth it.

In my determination to avoid Tashinga and reach the Ume as soon as I possibly could, my concentration wavered and that can so easily be fatal in the bush. At one stage I found myself deep in a patch of extremely thick jess bush, which was a decidedly uncomfortable place to be.

Jess, or jesse as it is sometimes known is no particular variety of forest but occurs when trees, bushes and ground foliage grow thickly together, forming a dense wall of vegetation, impenetrable to all but the most horny-hided of creatures. Not even a self respecting lizard would venture into jess bush unless he really had no choice. The name comes from the Chichewa word '*pa jesi'* which literally translated means 'you can't go there' and believe me, in normal circumstances, you can't.

But these were not normal circumstances. I was frightened, weary, hot and in a hurry. I had blundered into the jess and although it would have been far more sensible to back my way carefully out of it, I wasn't thinking straight so just pushed on through the trees, creepers, foliage and bushes that blocked my path. Branches – some of them evilly thorned – tore at my clothing and my exposed skin. Blood ran down my arms, legs and face to mingle with the sweat that was flowing off my body like a hundred little waterfalls. I had to stop on a number of occasions to ease my bulky pack through the tangle, frequently having to take it right off and crawl through, pushing the ruddy thing ahead of me.

It must have been about noon and terrifyingly hot when my walk to Binga almost came to a sticky end. I had no idea where I was or where I was going. I didn't have the energy or perhaps the initiative to check my compass and for all I knew I might have been heading directly for the front office at Tashinga, but I no longer cared. I had been in the jess for nearly an hour and I had had enough. This wasn't fun. This was pure self-inflicted torture and I wanted to sit down and bawl my eyes out.

Without any warning whatsoever, a lioness jumped up from almost beneath my feet. She must have been two metres from me and fortunately, she ran off in the opposite direction. I stopped and so did my heart as another huge cat followed the first, then another and then another. Swivelling my eyes but not moving anything else, I looked around for more and found myself gazing deep into a pair of huge yellow orbs that seemed to hold an almost thoughtful expression.

This lioness had no intention of moving and she lay in the undergrowth about four metres to my right. Her haunches were vaguely visible through the tangled foliage but her head and shoulders were in plain view and terrifying for their sheer size and the awesome power they projected. With my brain suddenly clear, I could smell her feral scent and both see and hear the flies buzzing around her muzzle. I don't know how long we looked into each other's eyes but at that moment, there was nothing else for me in the entire universe. I was almost within touching distance of one of the largest and most dangerous animals in the world and if she felt like it, she could kill me without raising a sweat. It was not a pleasant thought.

This time I had to reverse. If I didn't, I would die. That was all there was to it. Moving with infinite caution, I put one foot behind me and began the slowest and most frightening backward walk of my life. Tangled branches tore at the back of my neck and I heard one sleeve of my shirt rip with a sound like the starter motor of a chainsaw. I paused but those implacable eyes were still fixed on me and the lioness hadn't even blinked. I held her gaze as steadily as I could.

There are many theories as to how one faces down a lion. Some experts advise people not to look at them. 'Allow them to feel dominant,' they say. I have never agreed with that. I felt that I had to impose my own dominance even though I was a curdling mass of funk inside. I had to make her stay where she was and to do that, I had to stare her down.

That long reverse seemed to take an age but I don't suppose it did. Even when I couldn't see that huge head any longer, I continued with my slow backward paces, trying to make as little sound as possible. At last my nerves snapped and I could take it no longer. Whirling around I pushed my way through the jess just as fast as I possibly could. Blood flowed freely, but I didn't care. I just wanted to put as much distance as possible between myself and that fearsome jungle killer. I didn't care about my direction or my comfort. I had to get away.

When I finally emerged from that awful tangle of vegetation I was a trembling wreck. Once again I had been incredibly lucky. I had blundered into that group of lions through my own stupidity and it was only the fact that they must have been well fed that saved my life. A hungry lion would not have hesitated to attack me and in that matted jess, I would not have stood a chance.

Sitting in the sparse shade of two tall mopani trees, I drank thirstily from a muddy spring and tried to control my fluttering nerves and trembling hands. I felt sick with reaction. I was too damned old to put myself through all this but there was still an awfully long way to go.

I had done it. I was through the park. I had a huge feeling of relief as I sat on a rock for my evening pipe. The Ume river lay sultry and swollen in front of me and on the far side, I could see lights coming on at the crocodile farm. After the hardships, fears and frights of the previous week, those lights offered comfort and security. They offered normality. They also offered the possibility of proper food. My meals in a mug were now boring me to tears and I didn't think they were doing me much good. Perhaps I should have listened to those folk who had cautioned against them as not containing much in the way of vitamins or sustenance.

Gazing out on that wonderful river, I couldn't make up my mind whether I was in good condition or not. I was certainly a great deal fitter and stronger than I had been when I started off, but I was suffering ever more frequent attacks of dizziness and despite the hardness of my newly developed muscles, my pack still seemed awfully heavy when I swung it on to my shoulders.

My stomach was playing up and the cuts and scratches received when I pushed my way through the jess were already beginning to fester. I bathed them with tea tree oil but I didn't have enough elastoplast to cover them all, so whatever was in the medication was being forced to fight an unending battle with flies and a myriad other little monsters feasting on my caked blood.

The one small surprise was that so far I had not had any real problem with mosquitoes. I had brought a net with me but it remained in its covering and hadn't been used. Nor had I used my bivvy. I've always had a horror of sleeping in small tents so whenever I travel, I carry a bivvy as protection against the weather. This is a rectangular sheet of supposedly waterproof (I had my doubts) material with strings at each corner and across the middle. It did keep the rain off and as I sat beside the river on that sultry evening, I couldn't help wondering why I hadn't used it as a sun shelter instead of relying on the sparse shade cast by individual trees. For that matter, why hadn't I brought an umbrella with me? Local people used brollies in town on the hottest and driest days and it was not for their water proofing qualities. Even a small umbrella would have provided me with enough shade to keep the sun off my head and face.

But it was too late to worry about that now and my next problem was to find transport across the Ume

River. I was sure I could find a houseboat in one of the bays upstream and I fell asleep that night feeling very pleased with myself.

Probably more by luck than judgement, I had walked right around park headquarters at Tashinga, I had survived an incredibly close encounter with lions in the jess and assuming that I could cross the river on the morrow, I would have come through the Matusadona relatively unscathed. It had taken me eight days and a lot of sweat but I was almost there.

That was an achievement in itself and even if the wheels fell off at that stage, with nearly three hundred hard kilometres behind me, I would surely have achieved enough to make my walk to Binga a success.

Or would I?

I felt remarkably good when I woke beside the Ume on a fine, sunny morning. The air was fresh and although my sleep had been disturbed by a lonely hyena serenading me during the night, I had slept well. There would surely be a number of Kariba houseboats waiting for me in the bays upstream. All I had to do was wander slowly south along the river bank until I came across a holiday group and then persuade someone to take me across the river.

The Ume is a wide, deep and incredibly beautiful river. I had wandered its length in my police days, often taking some of the prettier tourists for leisurely picnics in the official launch, revelling in the scenery, lonely bays, the bird life and the unfeigned admiration of my passengers. They had been heady days and provided many wonderful memories of a particularly spectacular African river.

This time it was different. I was not yet out of danger from park patrols or lions and I had to walk. The heat of the day soon built up to its usual crushing discomfort and the high banks and wide bays abutting the river itself made for some very difficult walking. I was soon drenched with sweat and with my lion encounter still horribly fresh in my mind, had to make continuous stops to wipe the moisture off my glasses. As hour succeeded hour and the kilometres unrolled slowly behind me, I began to wonder if I would ever come across a houseboat. Perhaps something had happened and the Ume had been declared out of bounds to tourists. Had that been the case I would not have known about it and my spirits that had been so high on starting out, began to drop down into my boots. Would I ever get out of this ruddy park? I was beginning to doubt it.

I followed elephant paths for a while, but they were narrow and tended to meander away from the lake at times and after two heavy falls, I decided to get back beside the water. How the elephant themselves managed to traverse some of those tiny walkways, I couldn't imagine.

I had been walking for three hours and was flagging badly when I came out on a particularly wide bay and there on the other side was a group of houseboats, all moored and looking very dilapidated. I recognised the spot at once. This was the Bumi Water Wilderness, pioneered by my old friend the late Geoff Stutchbury and since imitated in various parts of the lake by other safari operators. I studied the boats with interest before moving closer.

It was immediately obvious that Water Wilderness had not been used for some time. Awnings on the houseboats hung in torn shreds and the entire camp had a forlorn air of abandonment that was very sad. This was modern Zimbabwe. The world had been fed a continuous diet of horror stories as to the dangers of visiting the place and foreign visitors were no longer interested in holidaying in the country, even for the opportunity to stay in enchanted spots like this one.

Carefully following a wandering bull elephant around the bay, I edged closer to the group of houseboats. They all seemed to be moored well offshore but if I could pull one in close and climb aboard, it would at least allow me to rest in a bit of shade and might even provide me with a nice spot to camp. That would mean another day in the park but the comfort on offer would surely be worth it.

The elephant was not in any hurry and progress was slow. I stuck close to the edge of the water and at times, I sank to my ankles in clinging black mud but I was too tired to care. I needed rest and I needed shade. The sun overhead hammered down on my head and shoulders, making me feel weak, nauseous and even a little nervous. I had thought it would be so easy to cross the Ume, but all of a sudden I wondered if I would ever get over to the other side.

My mind must have been wandering a bit when I tripped over a mooring rope. Falling flat on my face, I cursed myself for a fool and stood up again on shaky legs. The houseboat itself was about ten metres from where I stood, so I hauled on the painter until the ungainly craft started moving slowly toward me. As it did so, I was hailed from the middle of the bay.

Dropping the rope, I would have run for safety but there was nowhere to go. I was on a muddy bank and behind me the ground rose steeply into a small hill. Small perhaps but far too steep for me in my weakened condition.

"*Hodi*," I called back. "Where are you?"

It was an inane question but at my shout, a small, wiry black man appeared from a houseboat in the centre of the bay. Had I been more alert I would have seen the tender tied to this particular craft but my attention had been focussed on the boat closest to the bank. Moments later, an engine puttered into life and the tender moved slowly across to where I stood.

"I am Crynos Sir," the little Tonga greeted me warmly as he grounded the boat in the mud. "I am the watchman for Water Wilderness and you look very tired."

"May I come aboard your boat please Crynos?" I hoped he wouldn't refuse. "I am indeed very tired and need some shade."

Moments later I was aboard a spacious houseboat and being introduced to Crynos' companion Elemony who studied me with obvious suspicion. I don't suppose wandering strangers were too plentiful in that enchanted spot and he obviously worried about my motives.

Nevertheless, the two men made me welcome and it was bliss to sit down in a canvas chair and take my mud-caked boots off, allowing my toes to feel the air again, My feet were hard and calloused where initial blisters had solidified and I revelled in the feeling of freedom once the boots were off.

My two new friends boiled a kettle for tea and after plying me with questions as to what I was doing, wandered off to confer together. My only worry at that stage was whether they would take me across the river in their little tender.

My hopes were soon dashed. It was Crynos who rather sadly broke the news.

"We cannot take you across Sir," he told me politely. "Nor can we allow you to stay here long. If any scouts from Tashinga find your spoor they will think you are a poacher and if they follow it here, we will be arrested and probably tortured to find out who you are. Rest for a while but then I will have to put you back ashore."

It was a bitter blow and my spirits plummeted again, but I could see their point and did not want to cause difficulties for them. Wearily, I bent to put my boots back on to my feet but Crynos stayed me with a gesture.

"You must eat first," he told me. "You do not look well."

I wasn't and although I felt far too hot and weary to eat anything, I knew it was good advice. Besides, every minute spent out of the blast of that terrible sun had to be savoured and enjoyed so I sat back and rested, wondering how I would cope when I had to leave that little haven.

Food when it came was boiled tiger fish with sadza – the stodgy maize porridge that is the staple diet of Africa. My English wife, Lace once told me that it tastes like wallpaper paste. The fish was delicious but the sadza stuck to the roof of my mouth and I left much of it. Crynos shook his head somewhat grimly when he took my plate.

"It will give you strength," he admonished gently but I waved him away.

"Sorry Crynos. I am just not hungry. It is too hot to eat."

He agreed that indeed it was terribly hot and we talked in desultory manner for a while. Despite the pristine beauty of his surroundings, the little Tonga was not a happy man. He and Elemony were awaiting resupply, which was already a week late and they were worried about their own food. For all that, they hadn't hesitated to share their meagre stocks with me and I felt even more guilty about wasting the precious maize meal.

During a period of contemplative silence, Crynos asked me what my surname was. I had introduced myself as David and told him that I was a writer. Now something was bothering him.

"Do you know Graeme Lemon?" He asked when I told him and I smilingly admitted that Graeme was my son. Without a word, he rose to his feet and left me alone, wondering what my younger brat had done in the past to offend this nice little man.

Not a bit of it. Five minutes later, Crynos was back with Elemony beside him.

"We will take you across the river in our boat, Sir." The quiet announcement made adrenalin flow through my system. "I worked for Graeme Lemon and he was a good man. We have agreed that we cannot allow his father to walk on in these conditions so we will take you over to the croc farm where we need to get some outboard oil."

The relief flooding through my system was almost palpable. From being in the depths of despair at the prospect of walking on up that now hateful river, I was back on track and would soon be out of the park. I could have hugged both men but the Tonga are not demonstrative people and I merely asked when we could go.

"As soon as you are ready Sir. We must be back here before it is dark and we want to move before any park patrols find your spoor."

He told me that they would do their best to obliterate as much of that spoor as they could once I was out of the way and when I offered to help, he smiled and pointed to my heavy boots.

"I think you might make it worse Sir. Leave it to us please."

I saw the logic of that and thirty minutes later, we were chugging across the wide Ume river in a Sport dinghy that brought back memories of Hobo and my rowing trip. The journey took nearly an hour but I hardly noticed the time. I was out of the Matusadona and for the moment at least, safe from park patrols and lions. It was with a feeling of enormous gratitude, not only to those two wonderful Tonga gentlemen but also to my son, Graeme that I stepped ashore outside the Ume Crocodile Farm and wandered up to introduce myself to whoever was in charge.

I had achieved another landmark in my journey and overcome one more of the huge problems that had been worrying me. The only thing that disturbed me now was that throughout my journey across the park, I hadn't seen a single buffalo and Matusadona has always been famous for its buffalo population. Nor had I seen a baboon and that seemed even stranger.

CHAPTER FIVE

(Delight and Disaster
at Nyanzirawo)

It was one of the most beautiful bays I had seen on my walk and I set up camp early on Saturday evening.

After a comfortable night with Jan and Mary Anne Dreyer at the Ume croc farm – I had to turn the air conditioning off because the noise was too much for me – I walked on the following day, my pack weighed down with home made biscuits and two large tins of baked beans, given to me by the kindly Dreyers. Finding myself back in light jess, I struggled for a while before spotting a well used path that took me down to Musampa fishing camp where I told my story yet again to a group of admiring Tonga villagers.

One fisherman called Shadreck took me under his wing but before we could do anything else, I had to be introduced to the camp chairman, Jeremiah. In the old days, he would have been the village '*sekuru*' or headman but in these supposedly more enlightened times, even everyday terminology has been altered to fit in with government ideals. Jeremiah had an office under a big tree and it consisted of a centre table and four large and very comfortable chairs, all made out of flat slabs of rock. I explained what I was doing in the Musampa area and with Jeremiah's assistant, who went by the unlikely name of Krugerand, I chatted about David Beckham of whom he professed himself to be a great fan. My knowledge of football is sketchy in the extreme but everyone has heard about Beckham.

'Had I met him,' was one of Krugerand's questions and he looked somewhat put out when I confessed that I had not. After all, Beckham and I lived in the same country so obviously such a meeting should have been arranged.

Apart from my shortcomings where football personalities were concerned, I must have passed whatever test I was being subjected to as after much weighty deliberation, Jeremiah declared that although I was perhaps slightly crazy – he used the Chishona word *penga*, I was obviously harmless and should be allowed to walk on without being handed over to higher authority.

Shadreck seemed as relieved as I was and after I had given him one tin of beans for his pains, he had his wife Beauty prepare us a meal of sadza and baked beans. It was all very civilised and when we were joined by a young man called Master who had also worked for Graeme Lemon Safaris, the party grew quite festive and I gave Master the other tin.

If you ever read this, Jan I am sorry but I have never enjoyed baked beans and they were heavy.

Shadreck and Master paddled me around the safari camp at Msango and dropped me off on the shoreline with directions as to how I would reach Nyanzirawo, so off I went again. It was not a hard walk as I had regular paths to follow. I was replete and felt pretty good when

I reached the bay and duly made my camp in a copse of small trees some fifty metres from the water. Once it was set up, I relaxed and sitting on my pack, enjoyed the majestic beauty of my surroundings.

Nyanzirawo really was a little corner of Paradise. The bay was wide and deep, surrounded by a heavy tree line and wide beaches, both of rock and of soft sand. A pod of hippopotamus frolicked and chortled on the side opposite to where I was camped and as always, the bird life was fantastic. Guinea fowl chinkled in the middle distance, a fish eagle shrieked its challenge to the world and an emerald spotted wood dove repetitively 'hoo hoo hood' from the trees. The entire area was surrounded by brooding, heavily forested hills. The Matusadona range was to the East and the smaller mountains of Bumi and Mola looked down on me from the south and West. I couldn't see the lake itself but this was a huge bay and I had more than enough water for all my needs.

Bathing on this trip was a strange but curiously satisfying process. I needed deep water where possible and my 'bathrooms' were invariably set in delightful surroundings. I would strip off, dive into the water, leap quickly out, soap myself, dive in again to sluice myself off and then let the sun dry me – all with a wary eye out for crocodiles. The whole process took less than a minute but would leave me feeling refreshed and pleased with myself.

Nyanzirawo was just such a bathroom and I smiled when I thought about the porcelain fittings and running water that so much of the world takes for granted. My bath had a backdrop and an ambience that could not be matched by man-made luxuries and in this bay, I had the additional advantage in that the water was deep right up to the edge so that I didn't have to paddle out of the shallows – always a nerve-wracking procedure.

After my bath, I settled myself on a big rock at the waters edge and let my mind and body relax, while behind me the radio broadcast an excited commentary on a premier league football match back in faraway Britain. I was content and wondered whether I ought to spend a couple of days in such a lovely spot. The trouble was that I was only a day or so from Chalala where I had promised to call in on Graeme's friends, Mike and Gail Otto and where I would probably spend a few days resting, relaxing and having my kit repaired. It seemed strange to have such a choice of leisure to ponder but I resolved to leave any decisions till the following day.

My reverie was interrupted by the hippo. To be more precise, one of the hippo - by the size of his massive head, the herd bull. Obviously curious about me or perhaps he was interested in the football commentary, he began moving purposefully across the bay in my direction. Anyone who spends time in the African bush grows accustomed to this. The leading member of any hippo pod will often approach, not only to investigate a stranger but also to demonstrate that he is in charge and it is sensible to stay away from the beasts in his care. This approach is not normally aggressive and usually ends with the bull fifteen metres or so distant and in deep water, where he will wiggle his ears, yawn to show terrifyingly massive canine teeth and sometimes give vent to that raucous laughing sound before rejoining his harem. It is a friendly warning and is invariably accepted as such. I watched this chap with interest but he did not behave according to custom.

Showing no signs of overt aggression and not moving at any great speed, that massive head moved steadily toward me – and kept moving steadily toward me. Worrying that the sound of the radio might be annoying him, I would have turned it off but it was on a rock some way behind me and to reach it I would have to get up and walk – which I had no intention of doing. Throughout my life I have been taught that if in trouble with any large or dangerous animal, stand still. In this case it meant sitting but the maxim still applied. Ignoring the commentator's banal chatter and praying that one side or the other wouldn't score a goal and thereby add to the decibel level, I watched that mighty animal approach.

Closer and closer the hippo bull came. Fifteen metres, ten metres, five metres – suddenly he was almost directly beneath me. I was probably one metre off the ground on my rock, but I think I might almost have been able to put my feet on that great head if I stretched my legs a bit.

It was an amazing feeling. Four tons of wild animal were almost within touching distance. I could see individual hairs on his muzzle and one huge brown eye swivelled to watch me as he drifted slowly past. Well, he wasn't really drifting; he was walking along the bottom but he seemed in no sort of a hurry. Allan Green of the BBC burbled on in the background, but for long pregnant seconds, that hippo bull and I might well have been alone in the world. It was a moment of communion with the wild that I had rarely experienced and never with hippopotamus. In a slightly nerve-wracking sort of way, it was truly wonderful and I knew I was enormously privileged. Suddenly the big fellow was past me and I watched with interest to see what he would do.

Ten metres beyond my position, the water obviously shallowed steeply and with a laboured grunt and a cascade of water from his flanks, the hippopotamus came out of the water. Ignoring my presence completely, he did what all mammals need to do on a regular basis, spattering the dung in all directions with his tail. Pausing like a winded athlete for a few moments, he turned slowly, eased his bulky frame back into the water and submerged until only his head was exposed. Then he moved back toward me.

Through it all I sat frozen to my rock. Moving away could have provoked him into aggression but to be honest, I didn't want to move. I have spent a lot of time among hippopotami but I had never seen one behave in such a manner. He wasn't aggressive and he wasn't scared. I suppose he was merely curious to see what I was, even though for once I should have smelled of soap rather than stale sweat.

This time the bull didn't pass quite as closely as he had on the previous occasion but he was still very near. Five metres away from where I sat, he paused for a moment, then opened his mouth in a wide yawn, doubtless showing off those mighty tusks and daring me to do something about it. The display over he rejoined his ladies, leaving me to expel my frozen breath in a gusty sigh and move back to my camp, marvelling at the wonders of Nature and thanking God for allowing me to share such a special moment with that hippo bull.

Relaxing in my camp, I boiled up a chicken and pasta meal, swilled it down with coffee and as it was the weekend, treated myself to a packet of fruit flakes.

Feeling very content and at peace with myself for once, I waited to see what further joys Nyanzirawo would provide for my entertainment.

I didn't have long to wait. The sun was beginning to set behind me when two female elephant wandered down to the water. They walked right past my copse of trees and it took me a while to realise that between them, they were escorting a tiny, knock-kneed calf. The baby was so young that it had liberal patches of pink skin all over its body and was covered with an overcoat of fine, reddish hair. It seemed fairly steady on its feet as it gambolled across the rocks with its two giant companions, but I wondered whether it had only just been born and was being brought back to be introduced to the family by Mum and the midwife. Unfortunately the light was fading fast and I wouldn't be able to witness any such meeting without leaving camp and moving considerably nearer. With a baby that young to protect, I wasn't sure that would be allowed.

Smiling to myself, I wriggled down into my sheet bag and prepared for sleep. I was comfortable and replete for once. I was making good progress and with luck would reach Chalala the following day. Stars were gradually winking into life above my head and a distant hyena howled to announce his present to the nocturnal world. What more could a bush wanderer want? It was moments like this that made my walk to Binga worthwhile.

But my excitement wasn't over for the day. Other elephants had joined the pair with the baby at the water and from the tree line fifty metres behind my camp, a single jumbo kept calling. I paid no attention to begin with then noticed that every time there was a shriek from the trees behind me, it would be answered by a gentle whickering rumble from the waters edge.

My camp was right beside a well used elephant path to the water and from the damage to the trees around me, it seemed likely that family groups would normally stop in the copse for a quick snack before going on down to drink and bathe. Sensing my presence, the majority of them were content to bypass the trees this time and were drinking and playing in the bay, but one youngster – and it had to be a youngster didn't it - wasn't having that. He or she knew that I was in the snack bar and was bellowing to the others to get rid of me. Every time he – I decided it had to be a boy – screamed his displeasure, Mum would answer from the waters edge.

'Come on down Baby. This chap is quite harmless.'

The thought made me smile and I lay there listening when suddenly 'Baby' decided that it was time to rejoin the family. I heard him start to run down a very rocky slope. Stones clattered at his passing and I could distinctly hear it when his feet slithered on smooth rock. Grabbing my camera, I focused it on a vaguely-seen gap between the trees and waited for jumbo to appear. As he approached the copse, his headlong pace slowed and I smilingly pressed the camera shutter as a huge, shadowy shape appeared in my gap. The resultant flash made him stop, turn angrily toward me and scream.

That loudly resonant trumpeting sound is one of the most chillingly awe-inspiring noises of Africa and normally when it is made above one's head, it weakens the knees and liquefies the bowels, but on this occasion, all I could do was laugh. After its challenge, the young elephant – the resultant, somewhat fuzzy photograph showed it was actually a female – ran on and moments later was back with the family. Chuckling rumbles and grunts told me that everyone was very pleased to see her and I rolled over to sleep feeling very content with life.

I would not have slept quite as well had I known that a major disaster was looming.

The sun rising over Nyanzirawo made a spectacular picture. Rays of orange, green and assorted reds seemed to flash across the water, skeletal trees shone white in the early morning light and a big crocodile looked quizzically at me from ten metres off shore. A small herd of impala frisked and played on the other side of the bay, many of them leaping high in the air for no other reason than that they felt like it. Smiling at their antics, I spotted a lone hyena wandering slope- backed and awkward through trees a little further away. He looked smugly satisfied with his night and sitting with my morning cup of tea, I felt at peace with the world. That feeling was not to last.

Having packed up camp I was ready to move on for Chalala, but decided to take one more picture to remind me of a particularly nice day and a wonderful part of Africa.

The camera would not work. No matter how often I pressed the on/off switch, nothing happened. In a state of mounting panic, I put new batteries into the ruddy thing but there was still no response. I checked the batteries in my radio and they worked perfectly so I tried again, carefully reinstalling them, cleaning the terminals and moving them around to ensure that they were making a good connection. There was nothing wrong with the batteries or the way they were installed. To look at, there was nothing wrong with the camera either except that it wouldn't work.

I was distraught. I needed photographs. Not only would they be essential if I was to get a book out of the walk, but they would provide memory fuel for many years to come and I needed that. My cameras had been soaked when I did my rowing trip so I had little to remind me of that little adventure, but the slides and prints taken while cycling down Africa still made me smile nostalgically when I browsed through them.

I wasn't even half way through my walk and I wasn't going to get any more photographs. It was a major disaster and I ran through possibilities in my mind. I could ham up some photographs after the walk was over but I knew they wouldn't look the same. I could get a lift back to Kariba from Chalala, buy another camera and get someone to drop me out again, but would anyone have a camera for sale and could I afford it anyway. I had brought a bit of money with me but only enough to cope with eventualities on the way and certainly not enough to buy a camera with cash. In Zimbabwe where electronic equipment of any sort was outlandishly expensive, I couldn't think of anyone who would part with a camera on the promise of being paid in time. Hell, I might be eaten by a lion along the way, in which case they would have lost an expensive bit of equipment. I didn't think anyone was going to take that risk. Somehow I had to get my own camera working.

But I couldn't. Although it was a fairly upmarket Canon and had done me proud over the years, it had definitely decided to give up the ghost. In my wanderings around Africa over the previous few years, I had swung it around, thrown it into the back of trucks and generally manhandled it. Now, in my moment of greatest need, it was getting its own back by dying on me.

With my euphoria of the day before completely dissipated and my soul skulking somewhere on a level with my toes, I started walking for Chalala. I felt it would probably take me two or three hours but it didn't seem to matter any more. Without a camera, my walk had little meaning. Without photographic evidence, nobody would believe my stories and as ever-advancing old age closed in, I would have nothing tangible to remind me of hot, hard but weirdly enjoyable walking days through wild, wild Africa.

It was in a state of acute misery that I moved into a small forest, vaguely noticing an elephant approaching from my left. The wind was in my favour so I automatically moved through the trees in front of the animal, but as I walked deeper into the forest, I realised that I had blundered into the middle of a herd.

There were elephant in front of me, elephant behind me and elephant all around me. One or two of them got my scent and a young mum came barrelling through the trees with baby at heel. I stood my ground and she stopped with a shrill scream before resuming her leisurely feeding. Baby looked vaguely bemused and moved underneath her body to suckle. It was pointless trying to walk on through the herd as I was bound to offend someone, so I sat on my pack and waited for them all to move away. They knew I meant no harm and I was certain they would leave me alone. Besides, they must surely sense my misery and know that I wasn't worth hassling.

It was a good half hour before those elephant did move on and it was a half hour that I would usually have hugely enjoyed but I was feeling far too down and far too miserable to enjoy anything. There were numerous opportunities for good photographs but of course, my camera was useless and tucked deep into my pack. I was angry with myself for not bringing a spare.

When the trees around me suddenly emptied and the bush went silent again, I hitched my pack back on to my back and wandered morosely on toward Chalala and a few days rest.

CHAPTER SIX

(The Angel of Chalala)

It was a beautiful morning and the going was relatively easy but I was not enjoying myself. The camera breaking down had shattered any enthusiasm I might have felt for the trip and after weeks of pain, suffering and struggle, I wanted to give it all up and just go home.

The big hill of Mola looked very close and there would be shops there but not the sort of shops that would sell or stock any sort of a camera, let alone a digital model. Somehow I would have to do the rest of the trip without taking photographs and then try and beg, borrow or steal vaguely relevant pics when I returned to Britain. It was not an enjoyable prospect and I felt very depressed as I walked on toward Chalala.

The old safari lodge at Bumi Hills loomed above me and I half smiled at the memories it evoked. What times we had enjoyed at Bumi Hills in those hard days of war. It was where we relaxed and let off steam under the benevolently tolerant gaze of an enlightened management.

Yet Bumi Hills had gone the way of so many similar establishments in Zimbabwe. Without tourism, lodges and hotels in remote places could not survive, no matter how much luxury and comfort they offered. Jan Dreyer at the Ume croc farm had told me that someone was opening Bumi Hills again and I hoped he was right. For a moment, I thought of having a look around the lodge for old times sake, but it would have entailed a fairly steep climb and the day was rapidly heating up, so I tipped a salute to ghosts of the past and kept moving

Walking along a wide dirt road that seemed to be heading west, I was lost in my old world of miserable worrying when I heard a vehicle coming up behind me. Moving into the verge I waited for it to pass but the engine noise dropped and a safari truck pulled to a halt beside me.

"Mr Lemon I presume?"

I bit back the withering retort that sprang to mind and smiled as big Alan Moodie climbed down from the drivers seat. Alan was a hunter, based in Kariba and had been a friend for many years. His pretty wife Vickie had been at Bronwen Blyth's sixth birthday party when I was hauled back to Kariba all those lifetimes ago.

We shook hands briefly and he complimented me on the progress I had made.

"Nobody in Kariba thinks you have a hope in hell of reaching Binga," he told me cheerfully. "They will be surprised when I tell them where I saw you."

He produced an icy cold coca cola from a cool box and offered me a lift to Chalala.

"Or would that be cheating?" he laughed and I shook my head.

"No I don't mind the occasional ride," I told him. "But I am only a few kays from Chalala and don't want to pull in there too early on a Sunday morning."

With a friendly slap on my shoulder that almost knocked me over, Alan jumped back into the truck, waved and drove off. I wondered what tales he would tell on his return to Kariba. The little meeting had cheered me up though and it was with a lighter heart that I continued on my way.

In 1967, sixty-seven thousand fingerlings of a Tanzanian sardine were introduced to Lake Kariba at Sinazongwe on the Zambian side. These little fellows, known as kapenta (*limnothrissa miodan* to the scientific types) obviously found conditions in their new home very much to their liking. The population expanded at an incredible rate and ten years later, the kapenta industry in Kariba was launched. The demand for the little fish was enormous and huge fortunes were made by those involved.

By the early eighties, kapenta were to be found throughout the lake and while Kariba and Binga were the main fishing centres on the Zimbabwean side, smaller camps and villages were set up and the ungainly-looking fishing rigs could be seen on almost every shoreline and in many lonely bays.

When I first visited Chalala, it was merely a deeply secluded bay with a small Tonga village in one corner. Remote and agonisingly beautiful, it provided safe anchorage for a number of larger boats and rigs so it was perhaps inevitable that it grew into a thriving little town. Stone built houses sprang up and velvety green lawns and flowerbeds, irrigated by an unending supply of water from the lake, enlivened the harsh dun colour of the surrounding bush. The huge bay became home mooring to many luxury cruisers and a number of the kapenta fishermen branched out into tourist ventures as a sideline.

It was still very much a frontier town however and life moved on at a leisurely pace. Everyone knew everyone else and if someone had a problem, friends and neighbours would gather round to assist. I had always enjoyed Chalala and as I walked down a small hill toward the entrance to Chalala Commercial Fisheries, I revelled in memories of good times spent in these cheerfully friendly surroundings.

Mike Otto was in the office and his eyes widened when he saw me. I don't suppose I looked particularly prepossessing in spite of my good bath the previous evening. I hadn't looked in a mirror for weeks but had no doubt that I looked wild, unkempt and probably dangerous. Gail looked over Mike's shoulder and confirmed my suspicions.

"My God!" She exclaimed. "You do look a mess. Come on in and have breakfast. We have guests today but you will enjoy them."

The breakfast was wonderful. Freshly caught bream, bacon and eggs, toast and all sorts of fruit, washed down with sweet tea. I tucked in with a will while answering questions from the Ottos and their guests.

Bill Taylor was a qualified dentist and he and his wife Meryl had been running a game farm in Matabeleland when they were driven off by Robert Mugabe's thuggish 'war veterans' in the land reclamation exercise.

"I hate to admit it," Bill laughed, "but it was the best thing that has happened to us in years. It brought Meryl and I here to Chalala where I can write and she can study her elephants. We lost most of our money when the farm was stolen but we have everything we need here and life is good."

It was nice to know that Robert Mugabe's brutal policies had helped someone.

Meryl, a former teacher of handicapped children was more interested in my walk.

"I bet you have some wonderful pictures," she said brightly. "If you are here for a few days, we would love to see them and hear all about your adventure."

Her words brought my predicament back with a bang and I confessed that although I did have some excellent photographs, there weren't going to be any more as my camera had 'died.'

"Batteries perhaps?" Mike put in from the other end of the table and I shook my head. I had tried all that. The problem lay with the camera, not anything else.

Meryl had gone quiet before suddenly turning to me and putting one hand on my shoulder.

"I have a spare camera," she said quietly. "Would you like to take that with you?

'It is digital and quite a good one."

She obviously misinterpreted the look on my face and turned away. I had known this gentle lady for less than twenty minutes and she was offering me an expensive digital camera to help me out of my awful predicament. I was about to disappear into the bush, possibly for a few more months and there was no guarantee that I would ever get out. Digital cameras were awfully expensive and hard to get in Zimbabwe so Meryl's offer was generous indeed.

"How would I get it back to you?" I stammered, not knowing what to say. My mind was churning with conflicting emotions. I wanted to accept the offer. I needed a camera. Meryl was offering me one but could I possibly take it? We didn't know each other and probably wouldn't meet again. It was a huge responsibility for me but the offer had been made.

"That doesn't matter," Meryl told me sweetly. "It was all meant to be. Why else would we have met like this today? If you don't get the camera back to me, I will survive."

I felt horribly tongue-tied and when Meryl pushed a big Olympus in its case toward me I wanted to cry. This wonderful, lovely, generous and truly nice lady had saved my walk from disappearing into oblivion. She had done it through the sheer goodness of her heart and I would have loved to throw my arms around her in my gratitude. I couldn't though. I had known her less than twenty minutes!

For all that, whenever I think of Meryl Taylor in the future, it will be with a great deal of loving gratitude and to me, she will always be 'The Angel of Chalala.'

The rest of the morning passed in a daze. I enjoyed the comfort and the abundance of food and drink but my mind still went round and round with the generosity of Meryl's wonderful offering. Perhaps it had something to do with the fact that she spent so much time with elephants. The simple generosity of the giant animals had obviously worn off on her.

Bill Taylor was a character. I had read his book, 'Wet Breams' and hadn't really enjoyed it, but he was a natural story teller and regaled us all with many hilarious accounts of his times in the bush. When I asked whether he missed dentistry, he laughed uproariously.

"Oh but I still practice," he assured me. "All the local Tonga come to me and I charge them one goat per extraction."

"How old are you?" He asked me at one stage.

"Sixty one and very nearly sixty two."

His craggy face lit up in an enormous grin.

"Thank God for that. I was sixty a few months ago and thought I was now too old to wander in the bush. You give me hope and renew my faith."

"You are only too old when you can't walk any more." I assured him and I knew I had made a friend.

Two friends really. Later that morning, I accompanied the Taylors and Gail down to the flood plain below Bumi Hills where I was introduced to Meryl's elephants. It was lovely to see the way the huge animals immediately recognised the truck and ambled across to say hello. Big bulls, teenagers, family groups and babies – Bumi Hills has always been famous for it elephant population and they all seemed to know the Taylors. Bill rumbled to some of the larger cows with his tongue and it was fascinating to watch the animals respond.

One particularly large bull took exception to our presence. Tossing his head in obvious annoyance, he advanced threateningly and stood with his ears spread wide. His trunk searched the air and he shrieked a blood curdling challenge.

"I don't know this chap," Bill murmured to me. "Meryl will calm him down though."

Meryl did. Speaking quietly to the disgruntled bull, she brought him back down to earth. I suppose it was the friendly timbre of her voice that did it but I could see that big fellow relax, the tension easing out of his system and the anger fading from his eyes. Moving hesitantly closer to our vehicle, he searched the air with his trunk and then, almost reluctantly pulled a tussock of grass from the ground, slapped it against one leg to get rid of the attached earth and chewed thoughtfully on the morsel. All was forgiven and we carried on with our little patrol.

Bill Taylor told me how he employed three scouts to collect snares in the area and later in the day, I looked aghast at a huge pile of the hateful wires stacked in one of his barns.

"That is less than a months worth from one small area." His tone was grave. "What chance do any of our animals stand under this sort of pressure? I just wish the various conservation organisations would speak up against this abomination."

We both knew they wouldn't.

With a camera – and a far better camera than my previous one – in my possession and a couple of days with very little to do, Chalala was a lovely interlude in my walk. Once again I was able to eat, drink and rest when I felt like it. Gail had a lovely library and I spent my time reading quietly under a huge marula tree in the garden. I had spent time in this same house after my rowing trip, only on that occasion, Mike's father, Hans had been in residence with his attractive wife Jeni. Now it was Mike's business and he was obviously doing well despite the economic problems of Zimbabwe.

There were two interesting characters working for Mike, with whom I spent a great deal of time. Karl Barnard was an overweight, bearded wreck of a man, terribly worried about his own health and employed as a sort of security manager. We shared a couple of whiskies while the Ottos were away in Kariba and after he had told me how sad his life was, it turned out that he had been an armourer in the police Support Unit during the last few years of the bush war. I had been a troop commander in the Unit in those days and although the name was vaguely familiar, I couldn't remember Karl at all. Mind you, his appearance would have certainly changed somewhat drastically since those proud days when the Black Boots, as we were known were an elite fighting unit.

Karl's monthly wage was less than a pittance but he assured me that having a roof over his head and being vaguely part of the Otto family more than made up for any lack of money. Life had not been good to Karl Barnard but I soon discovered that he was a mine of information on trees, plants and the uses of various herbs in the bush. I suggested that he should write a booklet on the subject and after greeting the suggestion with a deep frown, he brightened as the idea took root.

"Will you help me?" He asked and before I left Chalala I wrote out guidelines for him to use in his writing. I can only hope it gave him some focus for a life that seemed to be drifting gently into a lonely old age.

On my second morning in Chalala, I was reading quietly when a tall, dignified black man approached me somewhat hesitantly.

"Do you remember me Sir?"

I studied him intently but had to admit that I could see nothing familiar.

"I am Kidzo," he announced gravely. "I was working here at CCF when you came through in your little dinghy so many years ago. We were both younger then."

Considerably younger, I thought to myself but shook Kidzo's hand with enthusiasm. It is always nice to be remembered, particularly in the context of a previous adventure. Motioning him to sit down beside me, we chatted at length about times past and present.

"I won't ask you why you are walking to Binga," he smiled at me and I nodded in relief. "I remember how everyone wondered why you wanted to row on the lake when it is so dangerous. You proved us all wrong though, because nobody thought you would survive that journey. It was a time of storms but you came through them all."

Wow! That was a lovely compliment and made me feel pretty pleased with myself even though I could remember only a couple of those storms. I wondered what they all thought this time and whether I would be able to prove them wrong again.

That evening I went for 'sundowners' on the flood plain with the Taylors and a farming couple from Marondera. We enjoyed drinks and snacks among elephants and buffalo. The animals seemed content to accept our presence among them. The sun went down in its usual spectacular fashion and all of us were quiet as we watched its fiery descent into the water. Kariba sunsets are surely among the most colourfully beautiful in the world and even though I had watched them every evening for the past month or so, every one left me feeling breathless at its sheer magnificence.

It was a lovely evening, but on our way back to Chalala we came across a tiny baby elephant with a snare stuck deep into its ear and trailing behind it. The poor little mite kept treading on the loose bit of wire and every time she did that, the loop of the snare would be working itself ever deeper into the side of her head. Meryl was distraught.

"It is Holly," she had named a number of the Bumi family groups. "She is only a few months old but we had to dart her and take a snare off only a few weeks ago."

That evening, she tried to contact Mark Brightman at the crocodile farm. Mark was the only person in the area licensed to carry out darting operations but he was away in Harare at the time. Poor little Holly would have to wait a few more days before she was released from that cruel loop of wire.

In the event, Holly's fellow elephants somehow managed to remove that snare but in one of those accumulated tragedies that seem to afflict individuals of all species, she later died in yet another snare.

By then I was way beyond Chalala and wasn't to learn about her death until many months later.

Chalala had been a wonderfully restful interlude for me. I moved on feeling considerably stronger and happier in myself. Gail had fussed over me like a mother hen during my stay and everyone else had been helpful in the extreme and full of good wishes for the rest of my walk. The straps on my pack had been repaired by a net maker named Mafuta – the name means 'fat' but he wasn't – and there had also been that incredibly generous gesture of Meryl's to alleviate my ever more jaundiced opinion of my fellow human beings. I left the little fishing settlement, determined that I would succeed in my venture no matter what difficulties I had to face in future.

And difficulties there would surely be. I knew that but at times when my spirits were really low, I would be buoyed by the memory of what had to be one of the most selfless gestures I have ever experienced.

Meryl Taylor really was the Angel of Chalala where I was concerned and even though she had given me a large bag of rusks and dried banana to keep me going along the road, my pack seemed considerably lighter when I walked on toward Elephant Point and the mighty Sengwa Basin.

~

Elephant Point is a luxury safari camp situated in the mouth of the Sibilobilo River and well known for the beauty of its wild surroundings. At the time of my walk, the lease was still held by my son Graeme, although he had emigrated to Australia and the camp was run by Mike Otto. I had last visited Elephant Point on the occasion of Graeme's wedding and I wondered what memories the place would bring back.

Meryl's camera proved much bulkier than my own and I eventually had to carry it slung around my neck and bumping against my chest. It was a more advanced model then mine too and its only drawback where I was concerned, was that it did not have a time exposure facility, so I couldn't photograph myself. That sounds somewhat arrogant but I needed photographs of myself for any publicity I might get once the walk was over. Whatever the problems, having a camera again and the supreme generosity behind the giving of it were undoubtedly the main reason for my lift in spirits.

In a weirdly masochistic way, it was good to be back on the road and alone again among my elephants. I had a lovely time at Chalala and could easily have stayed on until the baby jumbo was relieved of her snare. However, the inactivity was starting to get to me and I felt this horrible urge to be walking again. After all, reaching Binga was the focal point of my life and had been for the last few weeks. I just had to keep moving on.

In the event Elephant Point was another lovely inter-lude. There was a skeleton staff looking after the camp and once they realised who I was, I was treated like royalty. A bed was made up in the most luxurious of the lodges and despite my protestations that I didn't need any cosseting, solar powered lights were switched on, my hot water boiler was lit and there was always someone at hand to make sure I was comfortable. At my request, Maxwell who was acting manager bought me a fresh bream from the nearby fishing camp and I enjoyed a wonderful meal of fried fish with Meryl's dried banana cut up and cooked in oil as an accompaniment.

In spite of my need to keep moving, I spent an addi-tional day in E.P, wandering around and wallowing in memories. One evening I walked up to the viewpoint high above the camp, but when I looked westward, my heart quailed at the vast expanse of wild country that I would have to walk across over the next few days. Africa is a huge continent and it seemed that I was trying to walk across one of the widest and wildest parts of it. Feeling considerably chastened, I hurried back to camp and settled down to relax.

While I was in Chalala, Mike Otto asked whether I used a map when I walked, but I assured him that I didn't need one. As long as I kept the lake in sight and on my right, I had to be travelling in the right direction but Mike persuaded me to take along a laminated chart, covering the area from Chalala to the other end of the Sengwa Basin. Feeling that it might prove quite amusing to know exactly where I was, I accepted the offer but that map was to prove one of the biggest mistakes I made throughout the walk.

CHAPTER SEVEN

(The Stormy Sengwa Basin)

Sleep was becoming a problem. No matter how weary I felt at the end of a day, I would toss and turn for hours before dropping off. Then I was awake again at four with the dawn still some distance away. It seemed such a shame, particularly as I had started the trip sleeping like a baby. I seemed permanently tired during the day and that could lead to mistakes and accidents as I walked. I wasn't yet free of lions or officialdom and still had the most difficult part of the walk ahead of me. The terrain would get considerably rougher and if I wasn't concentrating, I was more than likely to suffer a bad fall or walk into something dangerous that might not appreciate my presence in its domain.

I saw a solitary bull elephant when wandering around Graeme's camp and while getting in close for a picture, thought back to one area where I disagreed with Meryl's theories on the species. She reckoned that elephant don't like people on foot, but I couldn't accept that. I have always liked to get in close to the big beasts and have never felt in any way threatened.

My own theory is that people tend to get nervous when they are unprotected and elephant sense this and react accordingly. I have rarely worried about my safety whilst among them and so have been accepted to the extent that I am often allowed close enough to touch individual animals if I felt that way inclined. Mind you, I have taken a few liberties with elephants over the years but I've resisted that particular urge so far.

Problems that were not yet relevant seemed to crowd my mind while I was relaxing at Elephant Point and it was irritating. I had also become very reluctant to kill anything, even mosquitoes or mopani bees. No matter how much they hassled and irritated me, I would merely shoo them away instead of swatting them, as I would have done a few weeks previously. I wondered whether perhaps it was because I was now an equally tiny part of Nature and could as easily be swatted by lion, buffalo, elephant or crocodile. I didn't want to inflict that end on anything else.

Of course it could have been just that the heat had addled my brain.

⚘

Having studied Mike's chart at length, I knew exactly where to go once Maxwell had dropped me off at Sibilo-bilo fishing camp in the E.P canoe.

Taking a quick bearing with my compass, I shook hands with my cheerful taxi driver and set off to cross a long ridge of land that stretched out into the lake. According to the chart, it was the last main barrier before the Sengwa Basin so I felt that once I had the ridge behind me, I was well on my way.

After walking for an hour I was lost. It had all looked so simple from the comfort of Elephant Point, but I hadn't taken long to go horribly wrong. Studying the chart again in the sparse shade of a big mopani, I just couldn't see where I was. There were a number of prominent-looking hills marked, but I was surrounded by prominent-looking hills. There should have been nothing between myself and the lake to the west, but due west of me was a series of high ridges that I couldn't see on the chart.

Once again the countryside was hardly conducive to pleasant walking. There seemed to be little flat ground and I spent my time forcing a path around rocks and through euphorbia cactus and a mass of tangled under-growth. Grass seeds stuck in my socks and once again, the amount of sweating I was doing forced me to drink far more than was strictly necessary. I had no idea where I was and might as easily have been heading directly away from water as going towards it. Willing myself to remain calm, I decided that if I bore due west, I would have to reach the lake at some point, so keeping my compass close to hand, I branched off yet again. Heavy, larva-like rocks had to be circumvented or walked through and my shins took a pounding from flinty edges. Once again, blood flowed freely and I couldn't help wondering whether there were lions in the area. The smell of fresh blood about my person would surely make me a tempting prospect for early lunch.

It was late morning when I came out beside a deep green stream flowing sullenly through heavy vegetation. The water smelled foul but I walked along one bank and suddenly found myself among straggly but obviously cultivated maize plants. There had to be a village nearby. There was no habitation marked on the chart so I knew I was a long way from where I ought to have been.

Hearing voices up ahead I made a cautious approach and surprised two young men at their toilet in a muddy puddle. They greeted me courteously enough and on hearing that I wanted to get back to the lake, they took me first to a deeper, fast-flowing portion of the stream where I could fill my water bags without too much fear of disease, then escorted me away from the water, eventually showing me a small but obviously well used path. This they assured me would lead to a road and that would take me to the lake although it was apparently a long way off.

At that stage, the distance didn't worry me, although I was a little concerned that the path in question seemed to be heading north rather than west. Still, there didn't seem to be an alternative, so thanking my guides, I went in the direction they had indicated.

Three hours later I was still walking. My legs were rubbery, my vision blurred and I was drinking water at a great rate, just to keep myself going. Early in the afternoon, I crawled under a bush for some relief from that hammering sun, but rocks, dust, heat and insects made it impossible to get comfortable and I soon started walking again.

As thirst, discomfort and the pain of overtaxed muscles bit ever harder into my being, my steps became slower and slower. The path had indeed branched into a road but it was gravelly and hard going, even in boots. When I reached a crossroads, I was at a complete loss. Which way was I to go? My mind was wandering and I didn't think to study my compass but even had I done so, I probably would not have been any the wiser.

Putting my pack down under what I hoped was a fairly odd looking tree (I would have to find it again) I walked on carrying only my water bag. The sun seemed to grow ever hotter but it was probably my own weakness increasing. I heard a voice at one stage and stopped to listen, only to go on with a silly giggle when I realised that I had been talking aloud to myself.

It was a very long time since I had been lost in the bush and it was not a pleasant experience. I suppose I wasn't lost in the true sense of the word because I was on a road of sorts, but I had no idea where I was, my muscles were in danger of giving out on me and my water supply was decreasing by the moment. As the afternoon wore on, fear burgeoned in my heart and I knew I was in real trouble. There were no vehicle tracks on the road and although it was in reasonable condition, it didn't look as though it had been used for many months. Nobody was likely to come along and rescue me from my own stupidity.

A vulture planed low overhead, its shadow causing me to look up abruptly. I had no doubt at all that the big bird had noticed my stumbling progress, realised that I was in trouble and had come down to check out what sort of a meal I might provide if things went really wrong. It was not a nice moment.

Panic was beginning to take over when I came to the top of a rise and spotted the sheen of water many kilometres away to my left. It was definitely the lake, but there was an awful amount of rough country between myself and that tiny glimmer of water. Once again I found myself torn between two options. I was heading north so if I went on, I would probably come to the lake in due course anyway, but I wasn't sure how long it would take or whether my water would last. If I struck out on a westerly bearing, I would reach that little bit of the lake I could see, but it looked a very long way away and I would not have the benefit of a path to follow.

Sitting miserably beside the road, I wondered what to do.

In the end, it wasn't really a choice. My pack was a couple of kilometres behind me so even if I kept going north, I would have to return for it eventually. I knew the lake was due west so all I had to do was return to where I had left the pack, take a compass bearing west and keep going on that bearing.

The only problem was whether my water would last.

Feeling sick and sorry for myself, I wandered back down that dreadful road and at last, there was my pack right where I had left it. Groaning as I swung it on to my shoulders, I took a very careful compass bearing, left the road and headed west, the compass clasped firmly in my sweaty little hand.

Twenty minutes later, I was pushing my way through jess bush again. Branches tore at me and snagged in my pack and clothing. Sweat streamed down my face and body, mingling with the blood on my arms and legs to provide a feast for wandering flies and other insects – of which there seemed to be an awfully large amount. Mopani bees fluttered incessantly around my face and I slapped irritably at them until it occurred to me that by slapping, I was expending extra energy and thereby making myself even more thirsty. I just had to put up with the irritating discomfort they caused.

I followed the occasional path through the jess where elephant or buffalo had wandered through before me, but all too often these paths seemed to just peter out, leaving me wondering what had happened to the great beast that made them originally. On other occasions, the paths veered off in other directions but I knew that I had to head due west, so due west I headed, even when it meant fighting my way through that evilly clinging tangle of bush.

Through it all, the level in my last water container dropped steadily. My heart hammered with rising panic whenever I looked at that transparent plastic bag, now clutched firmly in my hand rather than tucked away as usual in my pack. I was too tired and frightened to rummage in my pack every time I needed a drink, so I carried the bag and swigged as I went along.

I don't know how many hours I spent walking during that long, hot, horrible afternoon but it must have been a fair few. Sometimes I groaned aloud with the weight of my pack, at other times I yelped as a whippy branch or twig sprang back to slap me stingingly on my face or other bits of exposed skin. As evening approached, I was down to a few sips of water and my sense of pure blind panic was getting greater by the minute. It seemed inevitable that I was going to die in the bush and I couldn't help wondering how long it would take.

I didn't see it at first. I had come out of a patch of particularly nasty jess and had paused for breath beside a stream bed. I had crossed a number of these during the afternoon and had tried digging for water in one of them. All were starkly dry however and stream beds had become nothing more than irritating obstacles to progress. My vision was blurred and I felt sick but it suddenly occurred to me that something was different. Wiping sweat from my face I looked carefully around and there, almost at my feet was a small, scummy pool of water.

The feelings that swept through my mind can't really be described. I wanted to yell. I probably did yell with the sheer relief of finding that tiny pool. The water was green and looked foul, but I didn't care. I had my little-used purifying tablets to sort that out. It was water. I was saved. I wasn't going to die of thirst after all. It was a heady feeling.

Climbing down to the pool I couldn't help noticing that there was no animal spoor around it, which made me somewhat uneasy. If wild life avoided it, there could well be something seriously wrong with the water. I didn't care. Filling my belt bottle to the brim, I dropped two tiny purifying tablets in and added two more for luck. I then had to sit and wait for the tablets to do their work but ten minutes later, I was able to drink my fill and it was truly wonderful. The cool liquid washed away thick layers of dusty phlegm that had accumulated in my throat and brought a modicum of strength back to my flagging body. The sheer joy of the moment made me feel weak with emotion.

Whilst at Chalala, Meryl had asked me whether I ever prayed in the bush or was conscious of any divine protection from my madness. I wasn't sure how to answer. Brought up in a Jesuit college, Catholicism had been drummed into me from an early age but although I believed in some sort of a Deity, I wasn't sure that any formal religion had the answers. For me, modern religion has too many expensive trappings and I wasn't interested in that, whereas when I embarked on my silly little adventures, there always seemed to be some guiding hand that kept me from the brink of ultimate disaster.

Meryl had smiled gently at my somewhat clumsy explanation but seemed to understand. The conversation came back to me as I soaked my bruised and wearied feet in that heavenly water. What guiding hand of fate, God or anything else had brought me out of the thick jess right beside this little pool. The countryside around me was dry, harsh and quite obviously waterless, yet here I was enjoying the balm of cool water on my feet and drinking my fill, whatever the consequences might be.

In fact, I searched the area before setting out the following morning and my little pool was the only source of water for many kilometres around. I couldn't explain it but was very grateful to Whoever had made the arrangements to bring me out of the jess at that particular spot.

It had not been a good day but I had surprised myself with my own strength. With very few breaks, I had walked in searing heat and through some of the roughest terrain imaginable for well over ten hours. At the end of it, I was scratched to ribbons, bleeding badly and terribly weary, but I was alive and quite amazed at my own fortitude. I had probably covered close to forty kilometres – much of it in wrong directions – and had I had my head screwed on properly, that distance covered would have taken me close to the Sengwa River – almost exactly the halfway point for my journey.

It was a sobering thought but I suddenly felt far more confident in my own ability than I had before.

The almost miraculous luck of finding that solitary pool the previous evening was brought forcibly home to me the following day. After a night that seemed totally silent – perhaps I was so exhausted that I slept like a dead man – I walked westward again after my search for more water in the area. The going was rough with further wide belts of jess to get through but I concentrated on the compass bearing and after four very hard hours, emerged on the shoreline of lovely Lake Kariba.

I would never have survived those four hours on the few mouthfuls of water I had left just before I found the pool the previous evening.

Once again I had been incredibly lucky.

The Sengwa Basin is the widest and wildest part of Lake Kariba. Notorious for its violent weather, the basin has sucked many a large cruiser into its depths. I had challenged this part of the lake in a number of craft during the Rhodesian bush war. Since those heady days, I had sailed it in a thirty foot ketch and I had crossed it twice while rowing my little dinghy Hobo. It seemed that on every occasion I had been out on the basin, the weather had been foul and that beautifully awful stretch of water had done its best to kill me.

Now the basin stretched out in front of me and I couldn't help feeling vaguely smug that I was ashore and immune to its nastiness. It all looked so achingly familiar. Away to my right was the old wartime base of Paradise Island and further west were the two conical islets, laughingly known as 'the dog's balls.' I was on a broad swathe of shoreline that had been burnt fairly recently although new grass was already peeping through the black stubble. Impala, waterbuck and warthog congregated on the flood plain, but they were shy and would not allow me close enough for a picture. Small piles of bones here and there showed where even some fleet-footed impala had not been able to escape the flames.

Big black clouds were building up on the other side of the basin and I reflected somewhat sourly that I could well have done with rain the previous day. In fact, I had been desperate for it whereas if it rained now, I would have to put my bivvy up and that would be a chore.

My camp was deep in a clump of trees and relatively comfortable. I had water aplenty and the rigours of the previous day were already becoming just a memory, although aching muscles would keep reminding me of the strain I had put my body through for a while to come.

After a meal of asparagus gruel and croutons, I drank three or four cups of tea on one teabag, then settled down for an afternoon sleep. I had an awful feeling that I was back in hunting area and this seemed to be confirmed by vehicle tracks that went all along the tree line, presumably where hunters had been looking for suitable specimens among the impala herds. In fact, it seemed very possible that the piles of bones I had earlier thought of as fire victims, had actually belonged to animals, shot by hunters for meat or bait.

There were lots of elephant though and all through the afternoon and evening, I saw the big fellows moving through my trees and occasionally feeding out on the foreshore. It was a lovely spot and I was pleased with myself at having survived the previous day and reached a part of the lake I knew so well. I reckoned it would take me three days to reach the Sengwa River itself and then I would once again have the problem of crossing a major watercourse or making a long detour inland.

Pushing such worries from my mind, I enjoyed a dreamless sleep and woke, refreshed and ready for anything. I was almost half way there. Suddenly I knew I was going to make it. I had already taken so much. I had been arrested, suffered terribly with thirst, hunger and extreme heat. I had come face to face with lions in the jess and 'enjoyed' numerous other encounters with large and dangerous animals. I had managed to get myself lost and frightened and been close to giving up on a number of occasions. Nevertheless I had survived it all and was almost half way to Binga with over five hundred kilometres already under my belt. Surely the lake and its surrounds couldn't throw anything more at me.

I should not have been so cocky.

There was a great deal of heavy cloud about that evening and I inwardly debated the wisdom of putting my bivvy up. The only problem with the bivvy was that it needed at least six and preferably eight anchoring points for the various cords. This meant moving into thick bush, rather than lying in the open under a tree. Besides, for all its flimsy makeup, the bivvy was claustrophobic, so I decided to put it up only when I had to. There are times when I am a complete fool!

The stars were out in force when I slipped into my sheet bag after a pleasant evening of elephant watching. A number of family groups had walked through my trees and in the main, they ignored me. One pair of large bulls came particularly close, ambling across the clearing in which I lay, neither of them paying me the slightest attention. Hyena eerily whooped their plans for the night and in the near distance a leopard coughed throatily. A bark close by made me open my eyes without moving and I watched a bushbuck on the other side of the clearing. He had spotted me but had not the faintest idea what I was and after his initial challenge, he stood in silent inspection for a good four minutes before barking again – they sound for all the world like medium sized dogs – and tripping daintily away through the shadows.

Guinea fowl kept up an incessant chatter long after the day had faded away but I ignored them and despite my deep sleep of the afternoon, soon drifted away into dreams.

Rain on my face woke me up. Hurriedly going through my rain-at-night drill perfected in the Matusadona, I was soon ponchoed, dry and waiting out the shower on my pack. It didn't last long and fifteen minutes later, I was back in bed and surrounded by elephants.

The shower had prevented me from hearing their arrival but they were all around me and very close. The night was inky black and after all that rain, I decided it was quite possible that they didn't know I was there. Not a huge problem in itself, but it could become one if a careless elephant stumbled over me and panicked. Feeling that discretion was the better part of valour, I sat up in my bed and lit my pipe.

It worked and the elephants disappeared as if by magic. One moment, they were feeding all around me, the sound of branches being stripped and elephant flatulence loud in the darkness, the next moment they had slipped away and the night was completely silent. Elephant are like that.

I was soon asleep again but just before midnight, I awoke to a real storm. The rain was lashing down and despite setting all sorts of records for my rain-at-night drill, I was damp and dispirited by the time the storm died away. Cursing the world and my own idleness in not putting my bivvy up, I climbed back into a decidedly damp sheet bag.

An hour later, the rain was back, this time in a steady, soaking deluge. It wasn't a storm, but large drops of water cascaded down and there wasn't a glimmer of light left in the sky. Calling myself every derogatory name I could think of, I sat on my pack for the third time and waited for the rain to cease.

It didn't. One o'clock came, then two, then three. There was no let up in that steady soaking. Water was beginning to run down my neck and I was decidedly out of sorts. Feeling that anything had to be better than sitting there getting wet, I stood up, collected firewood and performed a miracle of the arsonist's art by getting a blaze going. It was comforting, not only for its warmth but for the light that it shed and throughout that long night, I kept adding wood to the blaze. Fortunately there was lots of it lying around and although I normally eschew large fires in the bush, this one grew bigger and bigger as the long hours moved slowly along.

When five o'clock came, I knew that the new day was about to dawn but there was little disruption to the darkness. The wind was blowing from directly behind me, taking the rain out across the basin but somewhat to my horror, as soon as daylight arrived, the wind veered through one hundred and eighty degrees bringing the whole damned lot back to saturate me again. It was an enormous blow but there was absolutely nothing I could do about it.

With the fire blazing happily, I made coffee, then more coffee, then chicken and pasta gruel, then more coffee. I smoked pipe after pipe to keep my nerves steady even though I was beginning to run short on tobacco. I had shared it out quite liberally among the Tonga I met, but looking through my very damp stocks, I realised that I would have to forgo my pipe when in company or I would run out altogether.

It was late morning when the rain finally stopped. The foreshore in front of my camp was inches deep in water, while gulleys and runnels that had been dry and hard the previous day were now rushing little streams. In the trees behind me, frogs started up a mighty chorus and when I wandered back to investigate, I found a pan that was full to the brim with muddy water and already had its resident frogs and tadpoles. The previous day the pan had been nothing but a circular patch of cracked dry earth and I could only assume that the little amphibians had been hibernating beneath it, waiting for rain to arrive and the pan to fill.

Trees dripped morosely in the dank atmosphere and although I had been longing for rain to alleviate the heat, this was too much. My kit, my clothes, my bedding my boots – they were all sodden and Meryl's camera was only dry because it had sat out the storm wrapped in my spare shirt and nestling uncomfortably against my chest beneath the poncho. The skin on my hands and fingers had wrinkled in the rain and when I held my palm up, it looked like a sad case of washerwoman's hand.

I wondered what to do. The camp was no longer a comfortable one, but walking on might prove hard going. Everything would be very muddy and I didn't want to risk a fall, even though the ground thereabouts was relatively flat. Besides, everything needed to be dried out although there was no sun to do the drying and the wind seemed to have died away once it had ensured that I was very, very wet.

At one point I was standing with my back to the fire in an effort to dry my shorts when I felt a sharp pain on the back of my elbow. I thought at first it had been caused by a flying spark, but on investigating, I found a speckled spider the size of a ten pence coin. The little so-and-so had bitten me and made my arm burn most horribly. I could only hope that didn't mean more trouble for my battered system.

The rain had brought flies and other insects out in force and I sat somewhat disconsolately on my pack, swatting at them and wishing I was anywhere else in the world. This certainly wasn't fun and once again I wondered why I put myself through so much trauma and hardship at an age when I ought to be relaxing with pipe and slippers.

By mid afternoon, the sun was trying to break through lowering clouds and both temperature and humidity were climbing steadily. I wasn't comfortable so decided to move on after all. Bundling all my wet belongings into my pack, I set out through the sodden landscape, wondering quite what I was doing. There was no need to keep going. I should have taken the opportunity to relax a bit longer, dry out my things and enjoy another evening of elephant company. Here I was, plodding on and feeling wet and uncomfortable when I could have been drying out in a relatively comfortable camp.

It didn't make any sense – even to me.

I do love mopani trees. They are so hard, so rugged, so redolent of Africa. They burn so fragrantly and for so long, imparting a very special flavour to meat cooked on their coals. They also make wonderful backrests for the weary traveller but I was beginning to discover that whenever I put my bedroll down, sat on it and leaned luxuriously back against the bole of a large mopani, the ruddy tree would have grown a sharp, spiky excrescence that was always level with the base of my spine. After my umpteenth stabbing, I wondered whether I would ever learn to check first.

⇒

After walking for an hour or two, I approached a fishing camp perched on a small knoll. It looked like a fairly large village but I was in no mood for company so slipped away into the bush and hung my blanket out to dry on the lower branches of a big pod mahogany tree. Laying out my groundsheet, I tried to sleep but music blared from the nearby fishing camp and soon began to annoy me. There is nothing wrong with African music. I enjoy African music on occasion and have been known to dance, leap and gyrate with the best of them. The only trouble with African music is that it is so damned repetitive and invariably played at full volume, so after twenty minutes of having my ear drums bashed by noise, I somewhat sadly repacked my kit and walked on again.

I went around the village (the chart told me that it was McKenzie's but I no longer had faith in the chart) cut through their football field and walked on into a suddenly sunny evening, looking for a nice place to make my camp. I found it on a little hill close to a couple of rivers that were flowing well after the rain. With a wry smile that was probably more of a grimace, I put my bivvy up and settled down to read beneath it. My clothing was still very damp so I hung it all up on nearby trees and wore nothing at all until the sun started to fall into the lake and the temperature began to drop.

I saw more elephant that evening as well as kudu and impala – including a number of bright little fawns, obviously born since the rains began. Impala mums have this wonderful knack of holding back on births until the rains have started and it means that all the pregnant females in a herd will give birth at almost the same time. It is comical to watch the little ones leaping and prancing around like bright golden, miniature adults. They scamper about like all small children and to see them *en masse* does wonders for the soul.

On the way down to collect water, I wasn't concentrating and stepped into a particularly deep elephant footprint. Of course, it was full of water so my boot – which had been drying well – and my sock - which had been dry - were both saturated yet again. It really had been that sort of day.

I was abed with the darkness as usual, determined to make an especially early start the following day. According to the chart, I was only a few kilometres from Mukuyu fishing camp and as that was relatively close to the mouth of the Sengwa, I hoped I would be able to persuade someone to take me across the river in a dinghy or canoe.

Quite why I was in a hurry, I didn't know then and certainly don't know now. I had told myself from the start that 'there is no hurry in Africa,' yet here I was wearing my feet down to the ankles by pushing on at far too fast a rate. This was supposed to be a leisurely amble through the bush, but I knew only too well that I was going so fast that I wasn't seeing or experiencing enough to make it truly enjoyable. Once again, my journal tells it all.

'*Why am I pushing myself so bloody hard? What am I trying to prove and to who? I must be making fantastic progress yet I have all the time in the world to finish this trip. I must, must, MUST slow down.*'

Needless to say, I didn't.

CHAPTER EIGHT

(Elephant Tragedy)

He was young and didn't seem to see me. I was sitting on a fallen log after an initial two hour walk through some glorious woodland when the man appeared, walking purposefully through the trees with one hand steadying a cloth-wrapped bundle, precariously balanced on his head.

I don't know why, but I didn't shout my normal greeting and merely watched in silence as he passed by some twenty metres from where I sat. I was fully exposed so could not understand why he hadn't seen me nor why I hadn't hailed him. Soon afterwards I resumed my walk.

It really was lovely countryside. The mopani trees were large and well spaced. There was little undergrowth and after the advent of rain, leaves were appearing on all the trees. In fact, the countryside was changing even as I watched. Two days previously everything had been stark, the mopanis skeletal and leafless, the undergrowth brown and crackly. Now there was a soft patina of green over everything. Almost all the trees were in leaf and my wild environment was beginning to look more like a benevolent old matron than the hard-eyed harridan she had been only a short while before.

I couldn't help smiling at the thought that if I was to study one closely for an hour or so, I would probably be able to watch a leaf grow.

Wild flowers too were peeping out of the most unlikely spots. What purpose did they serve in Nature's ladder, these delicate blooms? Pink, white and sometimes yellow, they smiled shyly at my passing, but their beauty would not be seen by anyone other than myself or perhaps the odd wandering tribesman, like the chap who had passed me earlier in the morning.

There was no wild life to be seen in this lovely forest but a woodland kingfisher was doing his best to drive me potty with his strident chatter. I had been hearing these birds – perhaps it was the same one – for days now and it was a sound that grated amid the peaceful tranquillity of my wild environment. Scowling into the upper branches, I yelled at my tormenter to go away, but he ignored me and continued with his clamour.

I didn't really mind. This was his home while I was merely passing through. Besides, I was feeling good about myself again. In addition to all the other hardships and calamities my walk had subjected me to so far, I had survived a ten hour rainstorm and felt all the stronger for it. After that little setback, I felt that I could take anything the lake and its surrounds could throw at me.

It was mid morning when I came out of the trees to find myself at the upper end of a deep inlet. In the distance I could see the man with the bundle on his head making his way in a wide detour, obviously following some well-defined path. I watched him for a while and saw him stop, place his burden on the ground and set about preparing a fire. He was less than a kilometre distant in a straight line and I decided to cut across and perhaps join him for a chat and a late breakfast. Having been walking around the lake for over four weeks, I should have known better.

All went well to begin with but then I encountered a small watery creek going right across my path. It looked quite deep and I found myself with a lengthy detour to make before it was narrow enough to cross. Veering toward the still visible smoke of the stranger's fire, I tried again and when I came to yet another flowing rivulet, took a running jump to get myself across. I was only a hundred metres or so from where I wanted to go and didn't fancy another long detour.

I landed in thick, wet and very black mud. The weight of my pack helped to drive my feet deep into this glutinous ooze and I felt the horrible stuff spattering my legs and body while flowing stickily into my socks and boots.

Calling myself all sorts of a fool for trying to take shortcuts and adding chats with wandering Tonga gentleman to my list of things to be avoided in future, I managed to clean myself up after a fashion. Still wiping sticky goo from my knees, I looked around for the man I was trying to reach. A little to my surprise, he had abandoned his fire, put his bundle back on to his head and was running as fast as he could go in the opposite direction. I wondered whether I had frightened him with my precipitate leap and spattering landing. It all seemed very odd, particularly when I reached his fire and discovered that he had left a cooking pot and small bag of mealie meal behind. I must have frightened him badly. I felt somewhat bewildered. Surely I didn't look that fearsome?

It was too hot to go on much further so I made camp on a narrow ridge that ran parallel to the inlet. There was a well-used footpath nearby and I decided that I was probably quite close to the fishing camp at Mukuyu. After doing a full laundry - quite apart from the muddy socks, my bedding still smelled damp and musty after the rain – under the scornful gaze of a lone hippopotamus, I hung it all up on branches, crawled under my bivvy and promptly fell asleep.

I awoke to find myself under interested scrutiny from a man wearing jeans and a blue shirt. Rising to my feet, I walked across to him and for a moment I thought he too was going to run. His eyes flickered past me and seemed to be exploring my camp. I introduced myself and asked what his name was. There followed that infinitesimal pause that policemen grow accustomed to in the course of their careers. It is a pause that invariably heralds a lie and I wasn't surprised when my visitor told me that he was called John – not an uncommon name and one that he would find easy to remember.

He was apparently camping on the opposite side of the inlet and when I pressed him for exactly where, he became somewhat evasive.

"Over there," he waved one hand expansively, "I am fishing with my two assistants and our boat is in the bay."

Where was he from, I enquired.

"Mukuyu fishing camp – that is where we are from. The fishing is not good at the moment so we thought we would try and catch small fish up here."

He went on to tell me that he and his assistants would be staying quite close to my camp that night as their 'operation' wasn't finished, but that he would escort me personally to Mukuyu the next day and help me get a boat across the Sengwa.

"We often go across the river for stores and beer," he smiled. "You will have no difficulty in getting a lift. I might even take you myself."

It was a wonderful offer and should have made me feel much better but there was something about 'John' that didn't seem right and I pushed him for a rendezvous time on the morrow.

"Uh.. early," was all he would say. "We will be here to fetch you when the sun comes up."

Later that afternoon, John reappeared with his assistants in tow. They were fascinated by my chart and were intrigued when I photographed them and then showed them the picture. Digital photography obviously hadn't reached that part of the Sengwa. Once again, John and his men seemed more than interested in my possessions and I resolved to sleep very lightly that night. As the sun was setting, I spotted the three of them walking away from where they were supposed to be camped and couldn't help wondering what they were up to. I had decided that they were probably itinerant poachers rather than fishermen and my trusty bush knife was close to hand when I did drop off to sleep.

It was while waiting for the worthy 'John' the next morning that my trip took an unexpected turn and my mood plunged from its high of the previous day to a feeling of deep despondency. The sun was high in the sky and I had just about given up on my erstwhile guide when I spotted a movement among trees near the water, some eighty metres to my right.

The movement was slow and ponderous so thinking that it was probably a hippo venturing ashore, I grabbed my camera and went across to see.

A baby elephant was walking slowly up from the waters edge. She was probably about three years old and looked very thin and out of condition. Her spinal column jutted from her back and she didn't appear to know what she was doing. With a quick but careful look around for Mum, I moved in as close as I dared.

Seeing me, the baby glared for a moment, then puffed herself up and spread her ears in challenge. Smiling at the threat, I called to her and she charged.

It wasn't a serious charge and when I backed off a few paces, she turned away. The poor little thing was lost and bewildered. I don't think she knew what I was and she was merely clearing some space for herself. I wondered what had happened to her family, as it was obvious that she was alone and had somehow lost the rest of the herd. It was desperately sad but is the sort of thing that occasionally happens in Africa. Mum might have been cut down by a snake or a snare, leaving the little one to fend for herself. Despite their close family connections, elephants seldom if ever adopt orphan calves and they are invariably cast out and left to die. That I was sure was what had happened to this little mite and for the first time, I wished I had brought a firearm with me. A quick death would surely be preferable to slow starvation.

But I hadn't and I didn't know what to do. I couldn't just abandon the baby but on the other hand, I was as helpless as she was. I couldn't feed her or look after her even if she were to follow me.

As it was, I followed her for a while, my camp, Mukuyu and the worthy John all forgotten. Still moving with infinite weariness, the baby led me into a dark thicket of big mopani trees, vaguely similar to the countryside through which I had walked the previous morning. I could hear frogs ahead and when the elephant paused beside a muddy pan from where the noise was coming, I saw the other baby.

This one was dead. Much younger than the one I had found, she had been killed by a spear thrust through the head and half the carcass had been butchered and removed. I wondered whether this was John's handiwork. It seemed eminently possible but then it could have been almost anyone. In fact, it might explain the curious flight of the young man I had seen early the previous day. If the bundle on his head contained illegal meat, he might well have taken me for authority and fled.

It wasn't difficult to picture the scenario with the baby elephants though. John or someone else would have come across them, obviously abandoned and would have immediately chased and killed the smaller of the two. The other would have run off, but they wouldn't be too bothered by that. Alone, it wouldn't run far and would almost certainly return in time to the spot where its little friend had died. All they had to do was wait for it to do that.

Of course, I was a bit of a fly in the ointment and suddenly I could understand John's questioning and wondering about me the previous day. My camp was less than a kilometre from where the baby had been killed and I could remember him asking me whether I was a policeman or from National Parks. No wonder he was worried if indeed he and his friends had been responsible for killing this little beast.

For me, the question was not why John or whoever had killed the elephant but why two babies of different ages should have been abandoned in the same place. That just does not happen. Africa is a harsh continent and there is no room for the weak, but I could not imagine any scenario that would account for two babies being abandoned by their respective mothers. Elephants give birth every four years or so and these two could not have been that far apart in age, so I didn't believe they shared the same mother. But if that were so, why would two mothers have abandoned calves in the same spot and at the same time? It was all very perplexing.

There was nothing I could do for the baby though. I watched somewhat sadly as she picked her way across a wide open area and winced inwardly when she fell while crossing a small gully. Such was the little elephant's weakness that she struggled to regain her feet and I uttered a silent prayer that John or other tribesmen would find her soon and dispatch her with their spears before she starved to death.

Feeling very despondent, I wandered back, packed up my camp and moved on. It had been a delightful spot to camp, but the enchantment had definitely gone for me. I had loved my walk down the wide, Eastern shoreline of the Sengwa Basin with all its wild life, birds and pretty flowers, but all I wanted to do at that stage was cross the river and get away from the place.

I could not get to sleep that night. The stars were out in force and the night noises were as soothing as ever, but my mind was in turmoil with visions of two sad little baby elephants. Why should there be two? That didn't make sense. One I could understand but two was too unlikely a scenario to be possible – unless of course two mothers had died in a fire or some similar catastrophe.

At about nine, I reached across for my water bottle. I always kept it beside my bed at night and frequently took a healthy swig when I woke for any reason. As my hand touched the felt covering of the bottle, one finger caught fire.

It was as if someone had driven a red hot nail up beneath my fingernail and I yelped with the pain. Hurriedly scrabbling for my torch I tried to find the culprit but I had taken too long and there was nothing to be seen. One harmless millipede, doubtless attracted by the light, wandered on to my sleeping mat and earned himself a healthy swat for his pains, even though I knew he wasn't the one that had bitten me.

A torchlight examination of my finger showed that it was already swelling up and the harsh throbbing pain was agonising. Knowing that sleep was well and truly gone for the moment, I made myself coffee and wondered whether to spice it up with a tot from my hip flask. The flask contained a single malt whisky and was strictly for medicinal or celebration purposes, but this was surely a medical emergency.

In the event, I stuck to plain coffee and a couple of paracetemol. In spite of my extensive first aid kit – I could have probably carried out an appendectomy or minor brain surgery - I had no idea what had bitten me so the bite, sting or whatever it was remained untended. All I could hope for was that someone in Mukuyu – if I ever reached the place - could suggest a Tonga remedy for extreme pain. Living permanently in these wild surroundings, they would suffer their fair share of insect

stings and snake bites so must surely know how to alleviate the mounting agony in my finger.

In the morning, the entire digit was swollen and
purplish but there was little I could do about it. As I was
painfully packing my kit, a little brown scorpion scuttled
from a side pocket of my pack and I had no doubt at all
that he was the evil creature that had bitten me. I have
never liked scorpions and the small brown ones are said
to administer a far more painful sting than their large
black cousins. I went after this little brute with a
vengeance, but yet again I was too slow and he disappeared into a hole in the nearest mopani tree.

Cursing scorpions, Africa and myself in equal propor-
tions, I resumed my walk. Two days later, I was still looking for Mukuyu fishing camp.

It had not been a good night. A hippo had come along to
investigate me at about half three in the morning and that
really destroyed my sleep. I hadn't been able to see the
brute, but I was obviously on or near his normal feeding
path as he came almost up to the foot of my bed and serenaded me for nearly ten minutes. The massive animal
growled, snorted, roared, howled and made assorted
sounds that were either expressions of extreme curiosity
or an attempt to scare me off without knowing what I
was. Perhaps he – or she for that matter – was eyeing me
up as a possible sexual partner. What a thought that was
but anything is possible in the African bush.

The hippo eventually calmed down and started feeding nearby. He was so close that I could hear powerful
teeth ripping at the grass and all I could do was lie still. It
would all have been funny if I wasn't so damned tired.

And now I was lost. I had been walking for a couple of hours and somehow managed to lose my way again. I could only blame the chart. It showed an old road heading directly for Mukuyu fishing camp and when I came across a wide but long disused thoroughfare, I promptly followed it.

The road on the chart might have led into the fishing camp but the road I followed went nowhere at all and after walking for hours, I found myself on the point of an empty headland. The lake was stretched out in front of me, elephant and zebra grazed in full view and the scenery was spectacular, but I didn't appreciate it. I wanted to reach Mukuyu. My finger was still painful and I was keen to get across the Sengwa River before anything else went wrong. However, I had no idea where I was and was faced with a choice of retracing my steps along the old road or going around the headland and walking inland along one bank of another very deep inlet.

A sunbathing turtle looked quizzically at me from a stump some ten metres offshore, but I ignored him, turned my face to the East – Binga lay to the West – and moved into the inlet.

It was a very beautiful bay but the hours seemed to pass extremely slowly as I plodded along. My heart was no longer in the trip and I seriously debated giving up and catching a boat back to Kariba. The drawback to that was that there wouldn't be any boats heading for Kariba. I was in the Sengwa Basin – arguably the wildest and certainly the most remote part of the lake.

I hardly noticed him at first. Everything seemed a little unreal and my mind was wandering, but I suddenly became aware of a man sitting on the prow of a beached fishing dinghy and watching me with evident curiosity.

"Good morning," I said politely and he clapped his hands lightly together in traditional greeting. "Am I anywhere close to Mukuyu?"

He must have recognised the name if not the words surrounding it as with a little smile, he gestured toward a steep bank that towered above our position. Looking up, I could see a cluster of small huts. I had arrived at Mukuyu without even knowing it and if I hadn't spotted the fisherman, would probably have walked right past the place.

Never does the old adage that 'There is No Hurry in Africa' seem more apt than when waiting for someone in a Tonga village. I had been told that the village chairman would have to decide whether I could be given a lift across the river or not and that he was out fishing. To my question as to the probable time of his return, I received a casual shrug.

"He will be back soon."

'Soon' could have meant five minutes, five hours or even five days and knowing that there was no way to hurry things along, I settled down to wait in a thatched shelter for visitors that was right in the centre of the village. With my back against a wall made from three-foot mopani poles and my body sheltered from the hammering sun, I was comfortable and relatively content. There were a number of men wandering about and many of them dropped in to talk or just check me out. One man called Moses could even speak English and we settled down for a conversation.

"Do you think there will be a boat going across the Sengwa soon, Moses?"

I was still anxious about crossing the river. Moses shrugged.

"I don't know," he admitted. "Like you, I am a visitor. I am only here to buy fish."

"What do you do and where do you live?"

"I am a cook for Ivan Carter Safaris," he told me proudly and I smiled in genuine enthusiasm. I knew Ivan Carter well. He and my son Graeme had been friendly rivals in the past. Each one ran his own safari company and they offered walking tours in the same area. For all that, they had been friends and as the two finest young guides in the country, they had competed to offer visitors the best safaris imaginable. I had heard that Ivan had gone into the hunting profession and I was interested to know how he was doing.

"We have a temporary camp only a few kilometres from here," Moses told me and I had immediate thoughts of a good meal and some convivial company. "Mr Carter is out today though. He has taken his client in search of a bull elephant. We shot two cows earlier in the week."

The last few words fell like stones into the deep pool of my mind. Two cows killed – two babies abandoned; it all started to make sense, but I would not have expected that from Ivan Carter. Tough and a wonderful bushman, I would not have believed that he could shoot two lactating cow elephants in any sort of circumstance. Yet that was precisely what Moses was telling me.

"Where did they shoot the cows, Moses?" I tried to keep my tone non committal.

"I am not sure but it could not have been far from here."

Deep anger boiled in my heart. I liked Ivan Carter. I had watched him in action and admired his casual efficiency, but if indeed he had shot the mothers of 'my' two baby elephants, he deserved prosecuting and having his licence taken away. It seemed to me that hunting in Zimbabwe was the only remaining profession to be making money but in the process, many professional hunters were forgetting all about the ethical side of hunting. I was brought up among hunters and although I could never bring myself to kill for money, I understood their love of the bush life and had always looked upon them as the finest conservationists of all. Now my ideals were being shattered. I wasn't sure what I could do about the matter, but was determined to write about it at the first opportunity. Those two dead babies – and I had no doubt that the second one would be dead by then – deserved to have someone tell their story.

My angry reverie was interrupted by a thick set individual who introduced himself as Keen Marumisa.

"I am the security officer for Mukuyu," he told me grandly, "and later today, I shall be going to Mirimsango business centre up the Sengwa. For ten thousand dollars, I will drop you on the other side of the river."

The price seemed somewhat steep for a trip that he would be doing anyway, so I offered four thousand and we haggled cheerfully for a while, eventually agreeing on six thousand Zimbabwe dollars – approximately three British pounds on the currency black market at the time.

Keen went on to tell me that villagers from Mukuyu rarely ventured across to the river as it was a long row and they had everything they needed where they were. He was merely taking his girlfriend – a stout lady who introduced herself as 'Mrs Moyo from Bulawayo' – to catch a bus at Mirimsango, a township well upstream.

When I asked whether there was a fisherman called John in the camp, he frowned in evident puzzlement.

"I know everyone in Mukuyu," he said proudly, "and we have nobody of that name. Why are you asking?"

It all seemed too complicated to explain so I decided that my meeting with John and his cronies was better written off to experience, although once again I had been lucky. I could so easily have been mugged, murdered or just robbed of my possessions and nobody would ever have been aware of it.

"I must have my hair cut before we go," Keen seemed quite happy with our financial arrangement. "We should leave in about an hour."

That suited me and soon afterwards one of the few women I had seen in the camp appeared with two hard-boiled eggs and a mug of sweet, milkless, Tonga tea, which she handed to me with a little curtsey. I clapped my palms together in gratitude.

It is an amazing thing about these hospitable Tonga people. No matter how poor they might be, they will always provide food for a stranger and I was touched by the gesture. Even without salt, the eggs tasted wonderful and I reflected on just how much I missed the everyday things that we all take for granted, without really know-ing that I was missing them. Two boiled eggs might not sound like much of a meal, but for me it was a veritable banquet.

Feeling replete and content, although the elephant story was still niggling in my brain, I wandered around the camp and wondered why civilisation was said to be such a good thing. The huts were small and basic, but each one had been individually decorated and one particular slogan emblazoned across a mud wall seemed to sum it all up.

'**Poor but rich,**' some philosophical type had written in bold black letters and I couldn't help agreeing wholeheartedly. These people had none of the amenities regarded as essential by people in the western world, but they were rich in the even tenor of their daily lives and the fact that everything was simple. They had no desire to accumulate wealth or be hugely successful in their work. As long as they had sufficient food, the occasional roughly-wrapped cigarette, friends around them and a reasonably comfortable home to sleep in, they were content and happy. This was surely how life was meant to be.

Tonga menfolk smoke whatever sort of tobacco they can lay their hands on, wrapped in clumsy-looking columns of newspaper, while their women are all pipe smokers. Not the normal pipes, known and loved in the western world, but pipes known as '*ncelwa*' which are made from hollowed out gourds. These are filled with water and a clay bowl on top of a reed is inserted into the gourd and filled with one of the most curious smoking mixtures that can be imagined. Tobacco is mixed with millet, herbs, an assortment of carefully chosen leaves and a goodly dollop of cannabis or *dagga* as it is known in Southern Africa. The smoke is inhaled through the water, as it is with the '*hookah*' or hubbly bubbly pipes of the Middle East. I had tried a puff from one of these pipes on my Hobo journey and the effect was a little like being kicked in the head by a particularly spiteful buffalo. For all that, the Tonga womenfolk are invariably heavy smokers.

There is little alcohol to be seen in Tonga villages although if the occasion warrants it, the women will brew 'seven day' beer in forty-gallon containers. The basic ingredient for this potion is millet but again, all sorts of other additives are included in the mixture and it also has an explosive effect on the unwary drinker.

Mukuyu was a typical Tonga kraal and there certainly wasn't any hurry for us to get moving. Villagers lolled about in the heat while one or two made half-hearted efforts to repair nets. Wandering among the huts, I couldn't help wondering how office workers in somewhere like London would view the apparent inactivity. They would probably be horrified at the waste of precious minutes, but I found it all vaguely reassuring. Thank God I am not the impatient type.

Keen's hour inevitably lengthened into two hours and then three but I was no longer in any sort of a hurry. At midday, I was given more food, this time a plate of boiled bottlenose and sadza. I had never tasted that particular fish before and although it was a little oily, it was delicious and despite my eggs earlier, I wolfed it down. Soon after I had finished the meal, Ivan Carter arrived.

I heard the truck first and then saw Ivan and two other white men walking toward me across the camp.

"I might have realised it would be a Lemon," Ivan shook my hand and I kept my feelings to myself. "My man told me there was a mad *marungu* (white man) walking to Binga so we came by to see who it was.

'Have you seen any elephants on your walk."

Suspicion curdled in my breast but I kept my tone even. There was no point in upsetting the man until I got to the bottom of the matter. Besides, I did not want to waste my lift across the Sengwa should Keen decide not to wait while I argued with the hunter.

"Lots of them," I told him. "I was quite surprised at how many there are along this shoreline."

We chatted for a while and Ivan kept shaking his head and saying how 'cool' it was to walk around the lake, but I was withdrawn and not enjoying myself. When he and his party left, they gave me a large bottle of coca cola. That was a kind gesture, but I couldn't help wondering whether they had called in just to find out how much I had seen on my walk. Ivan and his client would both know full well that shooting lactating cow elephants was not only unethical but also criminal and his questions about elephants all seemed very pointed. I was relieved when they drove away, although shortly afterward, the sound of a heavy rifle being fired made me hope that I hadn't brought them too much luck in their quest for another elephant to kill.

Keen Marumisa's haircut consisted of a careful shaving of his skull and plucking of whiskers from his chin but at last he was ready to go. I was relieved because Ivan's visit had unsettled me. He is a likeable man and although I didn't want to believe that he had shot the two mother elephants, the facts were certainly against him. Somehow those two babies had been orphaned and I could not think of any other possible explanation. It was with a heavy heart and a determination to do something about it, that I followed Keen down to his dinghy.

Tonga fishing dinghies are not the most comfortable of craft and when they are heavily laden, progress is inclined to be slow. I hadn't realised that the dinghy would be moored a couple of kilometres from camp and as a result, I walked there with my pack hitched uncomfortably over one shoulder. Keen set a brisk pace in front so – idiot that I am – I made sure I kept up and tried to breathe as lightly as possible without showing signs of undue strain when we reached the makeshift harbour.

I don't suppose anyone was fooled by my apparent *insouciance* but I stood watching in awful fascination as loading commenced. Keen's boat was one of the ubiquitous metal ten footers and I was a little anxious when I saw what it had to carry. I am not small and my pack was pretty heavy, but in addition to myself, we carried Mrs Moyo – even being very polite, she wasn't slim – and her luggage, a big bale of wet fish, another even bigger one of dried fish, Keen and his assistant paddler Amos plus their party clothing, taken along for a night in the flesh-pots of Mirimsango. Inevitably perhaps, there was also a live chicken, trussed and cast into the little pool of water that formed around my feet when I took my seat in the stern. It seemed an enormous load to be heading out into the lake with, but nobody else appeared concerned and I soon had more to worry about.

Despite the fact that I was a fare-paying passenger, I was expected to paddle, so wedged uncomfortably close to Mrs Moyo, I set to with a will. After less than a kilo-metre, we were forced ashore to bale out the boat which did little for my confidence, but at last we were out on open water, heading directly into the sunset and moving with painful slowness.

Although I was fit and strong after weeks of walk-ing, I was now using completely different muscles and was soon aching all over. My backside chafed on the hard wooden thwart and Mrs Moyo's ample bulk wedged my hip sharply against a metal gunwale. Water splashed agonisingly inboard with every plunge of the paddle and Amos was kept busy with the plastic baler.

The chicken flapped wearily in the gathering pool of water at my feet but there was little I could do to help it. Occasionally it let out an indignant squawk but nobody paid it any attention whatsoever.

Nevertheless we made progress and soon we were crabbing our way across the mouth of the mighty Sengwa. I looked on this as the half way point of my journey and despite my worries about baby elephants and unethical hunting practices, I was very pleased with my progress. The next section of the trip should be relatively easy and I wasn't expecting any real difficulties until I reached the Mwenda River and headed on into the Chete Hunting area.

That was still a long way ahead.

Overweight and not very fit

The road to Gache Gache

Worrying about water

The sunsets were magnificent

No porcelain fittings but what a lovely bathroom

These chaps made bathing interesting

A comfortable camp - note the bedroom fittings

The Angel of Chalala - and Bill

Young bull in the way

Tonga fishing dinghy -
stable but horribly uncomfortable

Thin and unhappy baby

Hot afternoon at the office

A free man in every sense

Simon with his waterborne carriage

Hard on boots and muscles

Beautiful Chete beach - and all mine

Sengwa taxi

'John' and his men study my chart

It is all over - cheers

PART TWO

SENGWA AND BEYOND

CHAPTER NINE

(Weary Days)

I could almost have been strolling around the outer suburbs of Harare. A wide dusty thoroughfare cut through the woodland around me and there was a constant stream of people walking in both directions. Donkey drawn carts passed at regular intervals and I was forced to stop on two occasions when cheerful herdsmen drove cattle down the road, obviously on their way to markets inland. Some of the younger men greeted me gravely but as usual, everyone seemed far too polite to ask where I was going or what I was doing in the area.

It was four days since Keen Marumisa dropped me off on he Western side of the Sengwa and although that particular landing had caused me some anxiety, everything worked out well in the end.

Although he professed to know the river well, Keen made a landfall on a small island and it was fortunate that I had walked on rather than set up camp, as was my original intention. It was only the ominous presence of a huge black cloud that kept me moving and when I came to a wide channel of water between myself and the mainland, I dropped my pack, ran back across the island and bellowed for my erstwhile taxi driver.

Amid much laughter and smiling apologies, Keen eventually put me ashore in the right place and I looked around for somewhere to shelter from the approaching storm. On a high bank above the spot where I had been dropped, I could see a small, neatly thatched shelter so I made for that as quickly as my tired legs would take me up the hill. The shelter turned out to be a lounge or recreation room on the edge of what appeared to be a safari camp. It was furnished with comfortable chairs and a table but all I was interested in was the roof overhead. Throwing my pack over a side-wall made of mopani poles, I wandered into the camp in search of a watchman.

It was getting dark and as I rounded a building, I was confronted by two men, one of whom had a shotgun levelled at my midriff. The other one who looked large and threatening in the gloom merely scowled at me.

"What are you doing here?" He demanded and I politely asked whether I might take advantage of the shelter to ride out the coming storm.

"Where are you going and why are you walking here?"

I sighed. I ought to have been used to this.

"I am walking from Kariba to Binga."

"Why?"

There it was again – the unanswerable question. There was no way of explaining it satisfactorily so I merely shrugged and muttered some platitude about it being a challenge. The big man was not impressed.

"This is a hunting camp," he told me. "You cannot sleep here. It is for clients only."

"It looks pretty empty to me."

I gestured at the obviously vacant buildings.

"I cannot allow you to stay here. You are not a client."

"Okay." It was his camp and I had to accept that, so turned to retrieve my pack. Shrugging it on to my shoulders, I walked back toward the two unsociable souls and paused for a moment when the big man spoke again.

"There is a fishing camp around the point," He jerked contemptuously into the evening with his thumb. "Perhaps they will allow you to stay."

It was dark and I was very tired so it seemed preferable to crawl into the trees and sleep through the rain, but I could sense the two men watching my back as I left them, so walked along the path that had been indicated. As I approached the point, I decided to peep at the fishing camp and perhaps shelter under one of their trees, slipping away well before first light. It didn't work out that way. I was suddenly challenged again, this time by three men (two black and one white) who were on their way down to the lake for some night fishing.

Again I went through my explanatory story and asked if I could sleep beneath a convenient tree, but Jan Pretorius wasn't having that. He arranged a bed and mattress for me, had the generator switched on (the noise was not what I needed) and showed me where the shower was. He then went fishing. As I was struggling to sleep – I was going through another bad patch, mainly because my mind was in a turmoil at the end of each day – it struck me that this had to be the camp, owned by my friend Corrie Pretorius of Johannesburg and his family. Corry had brought my brother in law, John Hammill to the place a couple of years previously and John had raved about it for ages.

It seemed a very strange coincidence, particularly as I arrived at the camp quite by accident. I hadn't even known it was there.

It rained hard through most of the night and well into the next morning so I was glad I wasn't out in it. Although I had encountered more than a little hostility from the hunting party in Gache Gache, I had met with nothing but kindness and hospitality since then so the reaction of the big man in the hunting camp had hit me hard. There has always been an unwritten law of hospitality to strangers in the African bush, but perhaps the man was a city boy, brought out to look after the camp. I discovered from Jan that the camp was owned by Ralston Safaris and the big man's name was Andrew so if any of the Ralston proprietors ever read this narrative, I hope they will impress upon their staff that the bush folk of Africa usually stick together and help each other when it is needed.

It proved another big blow to my already jaundiced opinion of the hunting fraternity.

Awaking in a comfortable bed the following day, I stood in front of a mirror to trim my somewhat tangled beard and conducted a general check of my aches and pains. My finger had subsided and didn't hurt any longer, my left leg was pussy and inflamed in one spot, but I was in pretty good shape. Dizzy spells still hit me from time to time but I liked to think that the intervals between them grew longer and I certainly felt stronger than I had for weeks.

I was losing a lot of weight though and that was disturbing. My hip-bones jutted out alarmingly and my beer belly had disappeared, while the top of my head was raw from repeated slaps and bangs dealt out by stray branches as I walked through tangled undergrowth. I didn't feel at all hungry but I had a hollow feeling in my tummy and smiled a little ruefully as I wondered how I would look on reaching Binga.

I spent a restful day in the Pretorius' camp, reading and repairing my kit as best I could. The sole of my left boot was close to the flapping stage and the right one had developed a hole in the leather above the heel. I managed to patch this up from the inside with elastoplast, but there was little I could do for the damaged sole without glue. I had a roll of strong cord in my kit so resolved that when the worst came to the worst as it surely would, I would bind the boot up with that and keep going.

The stitching was coming apart in various spots on my pack and I spent a few hours trying to repair it. My needlework was not exactly pretty but I hoped it would keep things together for a while. My spare clothing had accumulated a covering of smelly mould but I felt that could be sorted out by hanging everything out in the sun when it finally returned. For the moment however, rain beat a steady tattoo on the thatch above my head and much as I had longed for it over the weeks, I felt sneakily thrilled that I was under cover. I had almost forgotten what comfort was like over the previous fortnight.

I had a moment of deep introspection while stitching another rent in my shirt. What was I trying to prove and to whom? Most folk who knew me seemed to think I had lost my marbles and perhaps I had, but I somehow felt the need to test myself in my slightly crazy way. It was something different to my safe, secure and comfortable life as an English gardener, but I had probably taken on far more than I could realistically handle. I had done the same sort of thing in the past and possibly ended up better for it, but it seemed an awful lot of hardship to endure for no particular reason.

I knew I had a good brain but I seldom use it. I have always been physically strong but was reluctant to utilise that strength for anything useful. In fact I am basically an idle soul and usually shy away from challenge, hard work or pain. This trip was all three to the very Nth degree so I really could not understand why I was doing it. I didn't suppose I would ever be able to give a satisfactory explanation – even to myself.

Jan Pretorius was a little chap with shoulder length brown hair and a straggly beard. His eyes were sharp and he appeared to have become a little 'bush happy' in his wild environment. He gave me two meals during the day – and apologized for not feeding me on my arrival the previous evening – but his diet seemed to consist exclusively of boiled bream and sadza – filling but hardly delicious, particularly without salt. Quiet and generally withdrawn, he smoked newspaper-wrapped cigarettes like the Tonga and seemed more at home with his two camp staff than he did while talking to me. His hospitality was much appreciated though, particularly as it hammered down with rain for much of my stay.

Since leaving Jan – I managed to lose myself again on the way out of his camp – I had passed through entirely different countryside to anything I had encountered since starting out from Kariba. This was very nearly civilisation. I soon hit the main road from Mirimsango to the Sengwa fishing camp and knew from my study of the chart that it ran parallel to the shoreline as far as Sinamwenda and the start of the Chete hunting area. There was very little wild life in the area and I passed a number of small villages and settlements where the sound of dogs and chickens reminded me far too much of the world I wanted to leave behind. I dived into the bushes whenever I heard a vehicle approaching from either direction. Suddenly I felt shyer and more anti social than

I had felt at any stage of my trip. I didn't want to meet people. I didn't want to make conversation. I wanted to be back among my elephants and other animals, however dangerous. I wanted the simple life of the bush and the occasional Tonga kraal. I wanted peace and tranquillity, not the hustle and bustle of relative modernity.

I felt an almost overpowering need to get through that section of the trip as soon as I could. I longed to be back in the wild country for all its difficulties, discomfort and dangers.

The rain, which still came down at regular intervals but was welcome for its coolness had brought more wild flowers out and these soothed my somewhat fretful soul as I walked along. They seemed to grow singly in the most unsuitable bits of countryside, but sudden vivid splashes of colour were always nice to see. In one spot, I wriggled through undergrowth to photograph three 'fireballs' – a vividly crimson, spiky flower that I am told is part of the onion family. I wondered if anyone else would see their magnificent vitality before they faded away into oblivion.

My immediate goal was to reach Chipampa fishing camp, where I had enjoyed a lovely few days while rowing the lake all those years previously. I had been suffering from some sort of stomach upset when I rowed myself ashore on that occasion, but a little chap called Workington Nhari had made me welcome and gradually nursed me back to health. He had fed me, cosseted me, dosed me with some obnoxious medicine to cure my diarrhoea and throughout my visit, had never once stopped smiling. I had often thought about Workington and wondered how he was faring, so this was an opportunity to revisit the camp and find out for myself.

A bus rattled past me on a long, straight stretch of road and curious faces peered through the window at the lone white man with his big pack. I waved briefly then ignored them. A little further on, three young men stood chatting beside the road and at my approach, they separated and spread themselves across the thoroughfare, effectively blocking my way. I felt a sudden surge of anxiety. Was I about to be mugged? I would not have expected that sort of thing from the peaceful Tonga but this was the twenty first century and anything was possible. Carefully unclipping the retaining button on my bush knife I resolved to sell myself dearly.

I need not have worried. They were young but their smiles were broad as I walked up to them.

"We saw you from the bus," One of them told me. "Where are you going?"

"I am looking for a man called Workington Nhari at Chipampa," I explained. "He is an old friend who I have not seen for many years."

The name meant nothing to any of them but one chap, who introduced himself as Cephas Ntala took me under his wing and promised to show me a path leading directly to Chipampa that would save me a long walk by road.

Cephas was as good as his word. We walked through the huts and tiny terraced gardens of Mujeri village, coming out on a broad flood plain with the lake stretching away to my right. It was a welcome sight. For the past few days, I had been close enough to human habitation not to worry too much about water, but instead of filling my containers in local villages, I had siphoned the precious liquid out of puddles, elephant footprints and anywhere else it had settled during the rain. Now at least I could get it from the lake and I felt infinitely relieved.

Thunderclouds were lowering above our heads when Cephas bade me farewell and pointed toward distant huts on a small hill.

"Chipampa," he said briefly. "Good luck with your walk."

I gave him a gentle punch on the shoulder to show my appreciation and off I went again.

Chipampa turned out to be a huge disappointment. Not only had nobody heard of Workington Nhari – he was probably long dead – but the residents of the place were not particularly friendly. They seemed anxious to get me moving on and when I walked out of the village, a smell of fermenting beer gave a possible reason for their unfriendly attitude.

After twenty seven years of independence, I looked upon all Zimbabweans as equal, but in the remoter parts of Africa, a white skin is still seen as a mark of authority and not for the first time on this trip, I had the feeling that I was regarded as a symbol of that authority and therefore someone to be avoided when one was doing anything wrong. Brewing of beer had long been against the law throughout the country, but I didn't think it was looked upon as in any way serious. I certainly didn't care but I walked on feeling hugely disappointed that my welcome at Chipampa had not been as it was thirty years previously.

However, I was making excellent progress and getting ever closer to Sinamwenda and the wild country beyond, so there was a lightness to my step as I moved on along the path. Hopefully there would be someone at Sinamwenda who would be able to advise me on the best

way to get through the wild and horribly dangerous
Chete hunting area.

❧

The wire fence was covered with bougainvillea in bloom
and a lop-sided sign on the gate announced 'vacanceys.'

I smiled at the misspelling but didn't know whether
the vacanceys referred to were for some sort of bed and
breakfast establishment in the bush or whether it meant
that there was work to be had inside. Rain was threatening again so I walked in and approached a thin white
man in worn clothing who was bent over an old truck
with his head deep in its bowels.

"Good morning," I announced myself and he raised
his head to peer suspiciously at me through a snowy
white fringe that hung over his face. "May I take shelter
here and wait out the coming storm? In fact, could I
possibly spend the night somewhere dry?"

"I suppose so," his agreement was grudging but he
waved a hand at a row of thatched chalets stretching
away from what was obviously the main house. "Dump
your kit in one of those and I'll see you later."

With that, he went back to his recalcitrant engine and
I wandered down to make myself comfortable just as the
rain arrived. For the next few hours, it rained and rained
and rained. The temperature dropped alarmingly and for
the first time in weeks, I felt decidedly chilly. Wrapping
myself in my blanket, I sat on a low bed and looked out
at the heaving maelstrom that was still the Sengwa Basin.
I wasn't at all sure where I was but I was dry and relatively comfortable, so settled down to do a quick laundry and yet another kit and supplies check before lying
on the bed and reading my book.

As far as food stocks went, I was okay for everything except tea bags, of which I had just eleven remaining. I had bought eighty of them before leaving home, but they were in two packets of forty, so I must have left one packet behind in England. I felt like a total idiot. I didn't really deserve to succeed with my walk because in some respects, I had been ridiculously irresponsible. I needed my tea. It kept me going and lifted my spirits when other things were getting me down. I needed my tobacco too, although the shortage of that was due to my desire to share things with the Tonga rather than my own idiocy. It seemed a shame that both my little luxuries would have to be rationed when I had brought along so much to begin with – or would have had I not been so careless.

My loss of weight – though expected – was proving quite a worry. Curling up on the bed to keep warm that afternoon, I grabbed my thigh and could clearly feel the bone beneath. My arms also looked fairly stick-like and I knew that I had to keep my strength up somehow. A good meal or two would do the trick but I couldn't imagine my surly host at this particular camp offering me anything to eat. He gave the impression at our first meeting that he didn't want to know me and it was only my need for shelter from the storm that made me ignore his rudeness and take refuge in what was really a very basic and not particularly comfortable chalet.

I didn't see my taciturn host again until the evening. I had fed well on creamy chicken with croutons during the day and bought a packet of terribly expensive biscuits and a tiny tube of toothpaste from a little store adjacent to the property. An exploratory wander revealed that this was probably a kapenta fishing camp, occasionally used by visiting fishermen and I had no idea whether I would be expected to pay for my accommodation, although that did not seem to be of great importance. I was dry and I was resting tired muscles. That was more than enough to make my day enjoyable.

"Come across to the house and have a drink after supper," Phil Varkevisser appeared at the door to my chalet. "I have a bit of cane spirit left."

I think I might have preferred supper, but when I did go across, Phil was remarkably cheerful – in marked contrast to his surly demeanour of the morning. We sat on canvas chairs looking out over the water and like so many men who live alone in wild surroundings, he was careful with words but soon began to open up and tell me all about his life.

He was indeed a kapenta man but he usually lived in Binga while his family were in Botswana. He was looking after this particular camp for a friend of his and was reasonably happy, although the fishing was not good.

"Never a good time of year," he commented and I nodded wisely although I know nothing about catching kapenta.

After two cane and cokes, which went straight to my head, I told Phil that I would be on the road again the following morning, bade him goodnight and was walking away to my chalet when he called out to me.

"What time will you be leaving?"

"First light I suppose – provided it isn't hammering down with rain."

His long, lean face softened for a moment.

"Do you fancy a good breakfast before you go?"

I most certainly did and so my departure from that little camp – I had learned that it was Mwenda rather than Sinamwenda so I had gone wrong again – was delayed until the sun was high in the sky. By then I was comfortably replete with the nicest meal I had tasted in weeks. Eggs, bacon, sausages, beans; four pieces of toast and delightfully sweet jam, the whole repast washed down with buckets of coffee. It was a meal fit for any king and I was profuse in my thanks when I left Phil Varkevisser and following his instructions, struck out on a small path that would lead me to Sinamwenda.

"There are a couple of blokes there who might give you advice," Phil hadn't known enough about the Chete area to answer my questions. "They have been fishing here for years so will know far more than I do."

They would also have proper food and the prospect of tucking into another sumptuous meal or two was enough to keep me going throughout a long, sticky morning. The rain seemed to have disappeared but the clouds were heavy and low, pushing the humidity level up to an alarming degree.

Somehow I managed to get myself lost again, but shortly after midday, I walked into yet another Tonga fishing camp. The only person visible was a burly man repairing a net, slung between two trees. He looked up at my approach.

"*Mavuka biyeni,*" I greeted him in my best Chitonga and after a brief pause, his eyes lit up in a big smile.

"Oh I say," he spoke in beautifully modulated Oxford tones. "You speak Chitonga do you? How jolly clever of you."

I had to somewhat sheepishly admit that my Chitonga vocabulary was limited to three words and he burst into gales of snorting laughter. When I asked him – in English - which path I should take for the kapenta fishing settle-ment, he stopped what he was doing and escorted me through the village. Pausing in sight of the water, he pointed at a group of whitewashed buildings nestling among trees on the other side of a wide bay.

"There it is," he said cheerfully. "There are a couple of white fishermen there who will make you welcome, but I will take you there as it is still a long walk."

His name was Simon and ignoring my protest that I was quite capable of walking a few extra kilometres, he called for a friend of his named Kenias and the two of them guided me down to the water where he indicated a dug out canoe.

"Welcome aboard my water borne carriage," He said grandly. "She isn't much to look at but she is mine and I love her."

Simon had been brought up by missionaries and they had obviously been educated Englishmen if his accent was anything to go by. As we paddled across the bay, he regaled me with tales of his youth and told me that he had four first grade passes in Cambridge A levels.

"I suppose I should have headed for the cities and become a lawyer or a doctor," he laughed uproariously. "The simple life of a fisherman is all I wanted though, so here I am."

Before embarking on his fragile little craft, I had asked about the University of Zimbabwe research station at Sinamwenda but he shook his head somewhat sorrowfully.

"All gone now I'm afraid. Our revered President's suicidal fiscal policies made the place completely uneconomic and the university authorities abandoned it a few years ago. It is a tragic waste, but fairly symptomatic of modern Zimbabwe."

We were half way across the bay and I was desperately trying to keep my balance in the sometimes violently rocking bow when Simon yelled in my ear.

"The research station is behind your right shoulder," he called. "Would you like me to do a U turn and drop you off there? You will be in the forbidden area then and can walk on from there. It might save you a day or two."

It wasn't a difficult decision to make. I would miss out on learning more about the Chete area and the prospect of a couple of meals but I was well fed – for me - anyway and the opportunity to cross the wide Mwenda river sooner than expected was something I couldn't turn down.

Forty minutes later, the dug out grounded on a rocky shoreline just below the old university buildings and I stepped ashore into what Simon had so chillingly described as 'the forbidden area.' He and Kenias were the first boatmen not to ask for payment to bring me across and I was certainly grateful for their assistance. Scrabbling in my pockets for a gift, all I could find was my unused fishing kit which consisted of line, two floats and a few hooks. My two new friends seemed delighted with the little offering and waved somewhat anxious farewells.

"You be careful please," Simon called as he backed the flimsy craft away from the shore. "Keep well clear of park patrols. Those fellows will shoot you without even thinking about it."

I promised to be careful and knew that he was right. Even apart from the patrols, I was now heading into the true badlands of Kariba. The area was teeming with wild life and as the larger denizens of Chete would have been hunted to distraction throughout the preceding months, they were likely to be fractious, difficult and decidedly unfriendly.

Nevertheless, I was making good progress and with a final wave to the rapidly disappearing canoe, I turned my face away from the water and started into the Chete hunting area. This was where the real test of my stamina, strength and bush craft would begin.

I felt distinctly nervous as I climbed toward the research station.

CHAPTER TEN

(The Forbidden Area)

The research station at Sinamwenda was a huge disappointment and a tragic waste. The place was derelict, the buildings were falling apart and the miasmic stench of decay lay over the area so I didn't stay long. It was sad, particularly when I saw still-bottled specimens on a shelf in one building and rows of broken desks in another. How many keen young men and women would have studied and learned in that enchanted spot, enjoyed their time and gone on to great things in the wider world? How much potential still remained but would never be resurrected unless something extreme happened with the politics of Zimbabwe.

As a young policeman, I had paid many a patrol visit to the research station and remembered the days when both the university caretaker who lived at the bottom of the hill and the lake safety officer who lived at the top, were enthusiasts in the brewing of home made beer.

Any visitor in those days would be invited to sample both varieties and was occasionally served with two lunches, complete with home made wine. For me, the end result was usually a splendid day and a somewhat erratic path home in the big police launch. Both houses were now derelict and I felt sad as I walked through the wreckage of what had been a lovely place of learning and dreams.

In the lee of an old water boiler I found the remains of a fire that had not been cold for very long. Scraps of sadza on the ground around the ashes showed where somebody had eaten recently and I wondered whether the culprits had been a parks patrol or itinerant poachers. Whatever the case, it behoved me get away from there so with a last sad look around, I hitched my pack up on to my back and set off into the 'forbidden area.'

Moving on from the research station I immediately realised that walking was not going to be as easy as it had been on the previous section. Roads and paths were well behind me now and I had to climb over huge, rocky banks and work my way through ever more frequent areas of clinging jess.

In fact, the terrain was a real worry. If I were to fall fully laden with pack etc, I would undoubtedly break something and a broken leg in that remote spot would almost certainly prove fatal. Nobody knew where I was and there was no possibility of rescue in case of an accident. This area was just too remote and too wild. It was totally uninhabited apart from the occasional small hunting camp and these were all well inland. Park Headquarters at Chete itself was on the shoreline, but that was a long way ahead of me and I would need to avoid it in any case. I would have to concentrate on every step I took, which meant there would be no concentration left for lions, buffalo, unfriendly crocodiles etc – not to mention equally unfriendly park patrols and poachers.

I was well and truly on my own with no possibility of rescue should anything serious go wrong. It looked like being an interesting few weeks ahead and I somewhat sourly reflected that the rocks were not ideal treatment for my damaged boots either.

On the plus side, I was at least getting back into wild country again. Chete was famous for its elephant population and there was no shortage of lions, buffalo, leopards and other fairly frightening creatures. And crocodiles of course. Over the next couple of weeks, I would need to get through many long kilometres of deserted shoreline and if I didn't concentrate on spotting and avoiding those terrible armoured killers, I was as likely as not to step on one. Not the nicest of prospects.

I made my first Chete camp at the head of a deep lagoon behind Sinamwenda. The lagoon came off the Mwenda river and I knew I was a long way from the lake itself but it didn't seem to matter at that stage. I was into the most challenging section of my journey and it was a question of relaxing, taking stock and preparing myself for the ordeal ahead.

Checking the compass carefully before I set out the following morning, I headed north west and after crossing a couple of steep ridges, found myself forcing my way through thick jess. It was greener than I had been used to but long, whippy branches lashed at my face and all exposed bits of skin, proving every bit as painful as had the rougher, scratchier jess of the Matusadona and Gache Gache. Time and time again I was reduced to crawling through the undergrowth and in one of these tunnelling ventures, I managed to lose my chart.

I didn't notice the loss until the next time I stopped but I can't say I was terribly upset. I had been carrying the damned thing tucked between my back and my pack so it had obviously slipped out somewhere along the line. I smiled at the somewhat irreverent thought that the only creatures likely to find it were stray baboons. The thought of a big male *bobbo* sitting on a rock to read the chart made me smile although there was little to smile about at that stage. My arms and legs were dripping blood and I had obviously sustained a cut above my eye as blood kept trickling into it. After gentle days of walking along roads and well-defined paths, this was pure, self-inflicted torture.

It was frightening too. While I was on my hands and knees with branches lashing at my face, I was in no position to avoid the charge of any solitary buffalo wandering about in the jess. Apart from elephants and perhaps the occasional tiny duiker, buffalo were the only other creatures likely to be abroad in such thick vegetation and meeting up with one of them was a terrifying prospect. I was also quite likely to come across slumbering puff adders and they needed to be seen well in advance and avoided at all costs. I carried no anti venom kit – it would have needed to be kept cool – and a puff adder bite would have led to a slow, painful death.

It took me nearly three hours to reach the lake again and my heart sank when I found myself facing a wide bay, fringed with large, jagged rocks. Somehow I had to get around the bay and climbing over those huge stones was not a pleasant prospect.

I managed it eventually and after wriggling into some light scrub, set up camp for the day. It was still early, but it had not been a good morning. I had made a few kilometres of westward progress, but at a huge cost. I didn't mind losing the chart. It had caused me nothing but trouble and through my own stupidity and lack of map reading prowess, had caused me to lose my way on a number of occasions. The debilitating effect of forcing my way through that wicked jess was another matter. I felt totally exhausted and was bleeding from a number of new cuts and grazes on my face, arms and legs. My boots were suffering from the rocks too. The left one was almost in two pieces and I spent half an hour binding it up with green cord. It didn't look terribly nice but at least it kept the thing together.

My main worry was how much of this sort of punishment my system could take. The rocks alone were an enormous challenge. I had to keep watching where my feet went and the dangers of breaking bones went round and round in my mind. Some of those stones seemed like skyscrapers too. I am no mountaineer but there were times when I found myself inching my way up precipitous slopes, my nerves hammering and my spectacles misting up with the sweat dripping into my eyes.

I gave myself a long lecture at one stage when panic threatened to overwhelm me. I told myself to be patient and keep chipping away at the mileage. Even at that stage, it was obviously going to be a very long day as the sky was blue and totally devoid of cloud. Although it was only just after eight in the morning, it was already hellishly hot. Sweat streamed down my body and I felt quite weak and nauseous.

From what I remembered of this section of the lake, I had a great deal more of this punishment to get through too, so I was not a happy man when I finally fell asleep that night. It had not been a good day and I felt distinctly frightened about what lay ahead.

The wind was in my favour and the elephant had no clue as to my presence. The only problem was that we were on the same vague path and heading towards each other. It was only the fact that he was below me that had enabled me to see him before we collided and I glanced around frantically for a place to hide.

There wasn't one and eventually, I slipped my pack off, threw it hastily into the bush and climbed up a nearby mopani tree. It wasn't a large tree and I couldn't get myself more than four metres above the ground. My heart hammered as he drew closer. Would he see me? He only had to look up briefly and I would be in plain view but there was little I could do to alleviate the situation, so I settled myself as comfortably as I could and waited to see what would happen.

He was an old bull and in no particular hurry. Medium sized tusks jutted from his jaw and his eyes looked ineffably weary as he climbed slowly toward the point where I swayed precariously on my flimsy perch. Closer and closer he came. My pack looked frighteningly obvious but he ignored it. Stopping at the base of my tree, he paused for a moment that seemed like a lifetime before rubbing his gigantic bottom against that flimsy trunk. I clung on for grim life as the tree shuddered and shook, threatening to throw me out into the elephant's path. It was not a happy moment.

The sun was very hot and either the climb had tired him out or he was playing with me, but that massive animal suddenly leaned against my tree and fell asleep. I didn't believe it at first but his breathing grew ever louder and even above the noises of the bush, I could hear the rumbling snores begin. A grey lourie shrieked its 'g'waai' challenge in the near distance but I hardly noticed the bird and the elephant certainly didn't. I wondered what to do.

There was nothing I could do. I was trapped in my tree until the big fellow decided to move on. He slept and I waited. I didn't dare look at my watch for fear of alerting him to my presence, but time seemed to crawl by. Flies and mopani bees buzzed around my face, but I couldn't even swat them away. My muscles ached from the strain and I wanted to shout at the huge beast below me and tell him to bugger off, but that might well have led to rather nasty consequences. The tree had looked pretty solid from ground level but I didn't think it would stand up to an angry elephant.

Totally fed up with the helpless inaction of the moment, I finally tore a twig off the branches around me and dropped it into the centre of the elephant's back. He didn't move so I tried again. This time his ears flapped gently and he moved his head but he still appeared to be sleeping. A third twig brought a strange grunting noise from the elephant's throat and suddenly he was awake and moving again. With ponderous strides and what seemed to me like irritated flaps of his ears, he walked on up the faintly discernible track, leaving one heartily relieved wanderer in his wake.

It took another age before I regained enough confidence to climb down from my perch but when I checked my watch, I didn't think the entire episode had lasted more than ten minutes. It seemed like half a day.

Hours later when I was sitting on a rock with my evening pipe, drinking in the beauty of the lake and its surrounds, I decided that life really wasn't so bad. Birds muttered among themselves as they prepared for the night ahead and a bushbuck barked at something in the thick scrub behind my camp. Hyenas howled in the distance and a late-too-bed dove chortled in nearby trees. The lake, as well as the countryside around me looked incredibly lovely in the setting sun. Evening seemed to be spreading over the landscape like a softly coloured blanket and I had a feeling of deep peace in my soul. The water was calm; islands gleamed vivid green in the evening light and it seemed a tragedy that so spectacular a view was so seldom seen by mankind.

On the other hand, it probably wasn't such a bad thing, as the countryside was still pristine when daft wanderers like myself came along. It was an outlook to soothe the most troubled of souls and I felt inordinately privileged to be where I was.

Later on that evening I was moved to a burst of laughter while watching two squirrels playing together – perhaps it was a mating dance – in a tree close to where I was already tucked up in my sheet bag. One of them scrambled headlong down to the foot of the tree, examined my supine form for a moment or two, then launched himself on to my tummy and ran right over me on his way to nearby rocks. I breathed a silent vote of thanks to whoever was listening that he hadn't been an elephant or even anything remotely heavy.

It was at moments like that, I was so glad I had embarked on my silly little odyssey. After all, how else in our crowded twenty first century lifestyle would I have been able to sit within touching distance of a sleeping elephant?

⤐

Days spent walking through Chete were hard, wearying and relentlessly hot. The rain seemed to have gone for the moment and the temperature was soaring. I walked for hours with sweat dripping down my body and when I stopped, my breath seemed to burn in my chest as overtaxed lungs tried to bring themselves back on an even keel.

The countryside around me was spectacular. It was hard going, but there were times when I found myself on long, pink beaches that seemed to stretch away into infinity – and I was the only person around to see them. They were beautiful and all mine, but whenever I walked along that lovely sand, I felt totally exposed from both the trees inland and the lake itself. If a park patrol came along, I would not have a chance of hiding before they spotted me. It tended to mar my enjoyment of those beaches, although I still sat out beside the lake in the evenings. It was then that I couldn't help feeling that I had to be the luckiest man in the world.

At night it was different. Much as I enjoyed the spectacular vista of stars overhead and the wonderful bush sounds around me, worries kept crowding into my mind and keeping me from sleep. With only the Lwizilukulu (colloquially known as the Ruziruhuru) and Sengwe rivers ahead of me, I had crossed three of the five major obstacles to my progress. Yet all along I had been incredibly lucky and I couldn't help wondering whether this luck would last. If it didn't, getting past those rivers would necessitate long inland detours and I wasn't sure I could face that. I was fit, but I was very tired and despite liberal applications of tea tree oil and antiseptic cream, the jess damage to my left leg continued to fester. I could still walk but progress had become considerably slower with the increased pain around my shin and I did not want to go any further than I absolutely had to.

And of course there was the problem of National Parks. I had two official camps ahead of me, the first one at Siantura on the Ruzi and the next at Chete itself. I was confident that I could avoid detection at the former, but Chete was park headquarters and a fairly substantial complex perched on the edge of Chete Gorge. I would need to go a long way inland to avoid it and I was not looking forward to that.

All these thoughts and worries tumbled through my mind as I tried to drop off and on most mornings, I dragged myself out of bed, gummy-eyed and irritable from lack of sleep. I was enjoying myself and kept telling myself so but I wasn't sure how I was going to cope with the problems lying in wait for me.

The terrain seemed to become ever more brutal as the kilometres unrolled behind me. On more than one occasion, I found myself holding on to rocky faces by my fingertips, knowing full well that a fall would mean broken limbs and almost certainly a painful death. It was scary but certainly did wonders for my powers of concentration. I could almost understand the exhilaration mountaineers get from their chosen sport – almost.

Seventy percent of the shorelines were rockily rugged and the other thirty meant walking through thick, clinging sand – not particularly easy in heavy boots and weighed down by a gigantic (or so it felt) back pack. Long headlands jutted out into the lake and I occasionally tried cutting straight across these, but that meant being out of sight of water and often left me struggling in jess or thick bush where the prospect of blundering into something big was always in my mind. Occasionally I followed a long ridge of land that seemed to run parallel to the lake shore but although it offered easier walking, climbing up to it and getting down again were both exhausting and hazardous. I knew I ought to be walking in as straight a line as possible to minimise distance, but all too often I stuck close to the lake shore which meant walking around bays and inlets, often for many extra kilometres.

There was little wild life to be seen on the shoreline although I often found large concentrations of antelope and buffalo in the deeper inlets. They were desperately shy, with none of the friendly curiosity shown by their cousins in Kariba or further back along the lake shore. As soon as they got my scent, they ran for their lives and I cursed the hunting fraternity who were doubtless responsible for this state of extreme nervousness.

Mind you, I was becoming very much like an animal myself at that stage. I didn't move without testing the wind direction first. I walked with my eyes quartering the ground ahead for spoor and the bush around me for movement. If I moved out into the open, I spent five minutes checking the entire visible area for signs of anything out of the ordinary before making a move. I should think I smelled pretty animal-like as well. In fact, there was one morning when I awoke to a rank, gamey smell that made me think hyena had been about during the night. It persisted for a while and it was only when I put my jacket on that I realised that it was the garment giving off that foul stench. I suppose it was the accumulation of weeks of dirt and sweat. I made sure that I carried out a complete laundry soon afterwards.

There were times when I felt sad at the lack of animal life around me but I did see the occasional ele-

phant close to the waters edge and the beaches weren't
entirely empty.

⁓

It had been a long hot morning and I was ploughing
around a wide, U – shaped beach. Sand clung to my
boots and slipped with increasing frequency into my
socks but I had my eyes on a large, pod mahogany tree
on the other side of the bay.

Pod mahoganys are a boon for the wanderer. Even in
the dry months, they spread abundant shade and I was
only sad that there weren't more of them around the lake.
This one was a giant among the species and I looked
forward to a few hours of idle contemplation in the shade
cast by its heavily laden branches. I could see that shade.
I could almost feel it. The late morning sunshine tightened the skin on my face and arms but I didn't care. There
was shelter ahead and there was shade. I was going to
enjoy my day.

Nearer and nearer I came to the pod mahogany. More
and more did I revel in the prospect of cool (ish) relaxation. Birds chuntered half heartedly around me but
most of them were too hot to speak. I was hot too but I
didn't care. This was going to be a good day.

Fifteen metres from the tree and my hand moved
to the releasing catch on a shoulder strap. One flick
of a finger and the weight on my back shifted as the
strap sprang free. I breathed a deep sigh of relief
then froze where I stood at the briefest of movements
ahead.

Just beyond the pod mahogany was a patch of lush,
green almost knee-high grass. It was from there that the
movement had come and I stood stock still, my eyes

fixed on the spot. I hardly dared to breathe in the sudden tension of the moment.

Nothing happened. Was I imagining it? I didn't think so but the entire area around me seemed totally empty. I struggled to focus on the green patch. In the distance a fish eagle shrieked and I could hear the familiar repetitive call of the emerald spotted wood dove not too far away but I ignored all extraneous noises. I needed to concentrate. I wanted to get in under that tree but I had to know that the area was completely safe first. What was it that had attracted my attention? I didn't know but it behoved me to find out before I relaxed.

Sweat ran into my eyes but I didn't really notice it except as a minor irritant. This was far more serious. I needed rest and shade.

There it came again. The merest flicker of a tasselled tail above the grass and with a deeply felt groan, I hitched the loose strap back on to my shoulder. This was one pod mahogany I was not going to be resting under. I was too late. It was already occupied.

As I turned away to walk on along the beach, a huge, maned head lifted into view above the grass. The male lion watched me walk away, but he was far too sleepy and comfortable to pay me any more attention than that.

I am not sure how many of the big cats there were but as I left them, I heard the odd grunt from the grass and then a wide, careless yawn. The big fellow certainly wasn't on his own. I walked on feeling distinctly aggrieved but this was the bush and the lions were there first. I would just have to find another tree.

I did but it wasn't half so comfortable as that big pod mahogany. I was never keen on lions but that was the second occasion on which I had very nearly walked into them. I couldn't help wondering how long my luck would last.

Two days later, I found another orphan. An extremely young impala fawn stood motionless beside some bushes and it said something for my heightened bush sensitivities that I saw him at all. The little mite could not have been more than two weeks old and as I approached, he stood perfectly still, obviously thinking himself unseen.

With very young fawns, the mothers occasionally leave them in shade or thick cover while they go out foraging, but I should have thought this chap was old enough to walk with the herd. I had heard lions again the previous evening so it was entirely possible that mother had ended up as someone's evening meal, leaving baby to the mercy of the bush.

Not that there is ever much mercy on offer in the wild areas of Africa. It is very much a question of survival of the fittest and I knew that this little fellow was doomed. If the lions didn't eat him, something else would, but that is the nature of life in the bush.

Feeling sad at the waste of such a young life, I left him to his lonely watch and walked on.

To keep my mind away from its worries, I thought back to something Bill Taylor had said in far off Chalala.

"I read your Hobo book," he told me, "and I reckon you must have been quite down in spirit when you embarked on that little journey. Was it some sort of depression that set you off I wonder?"

Was it indeed? I supposed that I might well have been somewhat down at the time and perhaps that was the motivation behind my row, although I couldn't remember it as such.

On the other hand, perhaps depression is the motivation behind all my little adventures. Maybe I am merely running away from the problems of life? Thinking back on it, I hadn't really enjoyed the previous year or so and when I decided to do the walk I had so often promised myself, I really didn't care whether I made it or not. Dying alone in the bush seemed infinitely preferable to wasting away from the sheer boredom of my sterile life as a garden boy in England. In fact, I think I had started out with a somewhat childish 'at least I will be appreciated if I die' sort of attitude.

However, my views had certainly changed since then and I very much wanted to complete the walk, if only to show the doubters exactly what I could do and what I could achieve if I set my mind to it. In some ways, I supposed that was running away from my problems but it certainly didn't feel like it as I ploughed my way through the badlands of Chete. On the contrary, it felt worthwhile and if it was at all cowardly to run away from the humdrum reality of daily life, it could only be so in a very masochistic sort of way. Quite apart from the pain, traumas and tremendous challenge of walking across such rugged terrain, I was finding out ever more about myself and my capabilities, while at the same time, enjoying the solitude, the surroundings, the peace – and in a strange sort of way, the dangers and the sheer magnitude of the task I had set myself. It surely had to be good for me.

Or so I thought at the time.

CHAPTER ELEVEN

(Houseboat Hooligans)

I had stopped for coffee under a big marula tree and couldn't help looking somewhat wistfully up into its branches. It would be another month or two before the fruit would be ready to eat. A major problem in embarking on my walk when I had was the fact that at the end of a long dry season, it was difficult to live off the land. No fruit was out as yet and nor would there be any edible vegetation to be had until the rains had set in properly. The only natural food at that time of the year consisted of locusts, grubs and beetles – not really fare that appealed to me at the end of a long hard day.

I had enjoyed a meal of fried flying ants after one spell of rain but the effort involved in catching the little things and removing their wings was too much for me and I didn't repeat the exercise, even though they tasted pretty good. The same applied to fishing. There were plenty of delicious fish in the lake but after walking for a few hours, the last thing I felt like doing was going back out into the hot sun and sitting with a fishing line in my hand. Nor did I fancy the task of gutting and filleting the still flapping catch.

So I stuck to my meals in a mug even though they tasted increasingly awful and did not seem to be doing much to keep my strength up. To me they seemed more like gruel than soup or food, but they were all I had apart from a few remaining packets of fruit flakes.

Sipping at my coffee and enjoying the sweetness, I couldn't help smiling at thoughts of the previous night. There had been a big moon out and it must have been shortly after nine that I rolled over in my sheet bag, just as a leopard stepped out of the undergrowth and strolled unhurriedly down to the water. Although they are not by any means an endangered species, leopard are so shy that they are rarely seen out in the open so this was a thrilling sighting indeed.

The leopard was a big one – so much so that at first glance, I had thought it was a lion, but as the moonlight reflected off his magnificent pelt, I could almost count the rosettes. He – it was a male – must surely have known I was there, but it didn't seem to disturb him and I watched wide-eyed as he passed not ten metres from where I lay, my mind taking in the sheer magnificence of the cat and the arrogant, rippling power that make the leopards of Africa such very special creatures.

It had made for an excellent night but now I had a river to cross. My marula tree was right at the mouth of the Lwizilukulu and with a last check of the binding on my left boot, I turned inland and began to follow its course upstream.

The Lwizilukulu (literally translated from Chitonga it means 'big river') is more often referred to as the Ruzi and I knew the river well. I had rowed up between the steep, rocky banks. I had camped in an abandoned safari camp on Ruzi Island and ended up in the nearby parks camp at Siantura when a night adder had bitten me on the foot. I had endured days of pain and delirium but made new friends and been an awed witness when a pride of lions got among ranger, Piet Fick's chickens. The memory of a massive lioness standing on her hind legs to swat a squawking fowl into messy oblivion with her paw is one that will remain with me to my dying day.

Now of course, the parks camp would be enemy territory and rather than going there for help, this time I would need to get right around it without being seen. It was a prospect that preyed on my mind, as this was very wild country indeed and a favourite spot for lions.

It was hard going as I plodded upstream in the morning sunshine. I fell repeatedly among the rocks and each fall led to an anguished few seconds of wondering whether I had broken anything or seriously damaged myself. At one stage I heard an outboard engine and dived for cover as a small powerboat hurtled past. My worry was that the boat would belong to the parks department or that even if it was occupied by fishermen, they would have a scout or ranger with them as escort. I could not afford to be seen so I hid and rather sadly watched them roar on upstream. I could see fishing rods stacked against the stern of the craft so would probably have been safe but I couldn't afford to take the risk.

Ruzi Bay itself was as magnificent as ever. Roughly circular, it is very wide and it looked as though another camp had been built on the island in the centre. It was on that island that I had made the acquaintance of a big elephant that I christened Mama J. We had come face to face on a narrow path and my only fear at the time was that I would be forced to jettison a tin of pineapple chunks I had been looking forward to as my Easter treat. In the event, the elephant had given way and I could have kissed the huge animal. 'She' was actually a lone bull, but I had made her a female in order to give a punchy start to the relevant chapter in my Hobo book.

I couldn't see the Siantura camp but it was on top of a hill overlooking the bay so I had to stay in the trees to avoid being spotted by someone looking out. It made for heavy walking and at one stage, I came foolishly close to an old bull buffalo who scowled fiercely at me, probably not believing the evidence of his eyes.

Climbing down to the waters edge to refill my water bottle, I spotted the boat I had seen earlier. It seemed to be occupied by four white fishermen and I wondered whether to hail them and ask for a ride across the river itself. Before I could make any decision, they roared off again, disappearing up the distant channel of the river where it left the bay and headed south.

Cursing my own lack of resolve, I kept on walking. It was well after midday and I was wondering whether to camp for the day or try and make my way right around to the river when the fishing boat returned. I was sitting behind a small tree so they didn't see me and this time, they put their anchor down almost directly below my perch.

The boat did indeed contain four white passengers – all men - and I saw no sign of uniforms or parks insignia, so plucking up my courage, I climbed down from the rocks and approached them across a small strip of sand. Four pairs of startled eyes grew wide as they took in my somewhat crumpled appearance. I could imagine the stories they would be telling when they got home.

"Good morning," I said politely.

"Are you lost?" A voice called from the interior of the boat.

Of course I wasn't lost. I might have been a lost soul but I knew exactly where I was, even if I didn't particularly want to be there. Stifling an impatient retort, I asked if they would take me across the river.

"What for?" It was a different voice.

Here we went again.

"I am walking from Kariba to Binga."

There was a moment of two of silence that I am sure could only be described as 'stunned.'

"Oh," said the second voice. "Stay where you are and we will come across to you."

Moments later, the prow of the boat grounded on the sand and I swung my pack gratefully inboard.

"I am David Lemon," I announced as I climbed laboriously over the bow rail.

"Were you a cop?" The unexpected question came from a blondish man sitting in a fishing chair on the bow of the boat and I turned to look at him.

"Yes I was but it was a long time ago."

"In Marandellas 1978?

Marandellas had become Marondera in the new Zimbabwe but indeed I had been stationed there during the late seventies. I studied the man and he did look vaguely familiar.

"Paul Sheppard," he introduced himself. "I was in the police reserve and I read your canoeing book.

'This silly bugger," he turned to his companions, "canoed to Mlibizi and back again in the mid eighties. Now he is walking the ruddy lake shore. The world is surely full of dimbos."

He was smiling as he shook my hand so I didn't take offence and his reading of Hobo saved me making the usual impossible explanations as to why I was walking to Binga.

"In fact, I **rowed** the lake, Paul," I emphasised the verb. "Many folk have canoed it and I wish them all luck, but I am the only person who has rowed it in both directions."

I suppose I was being a little pedantic but even after all these years, I am still looked upon as 'the bloke who canoed Kariba.' My feat was worth far more than that as Hobo was distinctly more difficult to propel than any canoe.

"You had better come back to the houseboat for a beer before we take you across," Paul went on and I needed no second invitation. The mere fact of being out of the sun for a while was tempting but a beer as well? That must surely be heaven.

The houseboat *Abengane* was moored beside a river headland with another two tenders at her stern. As we pulled in beside the little boats, my heart nearly stopped. There, slung carelessly across the bow of a tender was an AK47 rifle such as are on issue to parks personnel. In the stern compartment of *Abengane* herself, a tall man in green uniform was chatting to the crew. National Parks from Siantura were paying a courtesy visit and I wondered what to do. I could hardly ask my new friends to take me back across the river now rather than later, particularly with the parks man looking on. Deciding to bluff it out, I slipped my belt with its attachments of water bottle, knife, compass etc off my waist and left both it and my pack in the tender.

Climbing aboard the houseboat, I greeted the parks man in Chishona and moved fairly quickly inboard. If he wondered why one 'fisherman' was overdressed in smelly khakis and wore heavy boots strapped up with cord, he made no comment, but I felt distinctly worried as I went up the stairs. My first beer tasted wonderful, but that taste was marred by a feeling of apprehension that I would be summoned to explain my presence before too long.

It didn't happen and one beer became two beers, then three, then lunch. Surrounded by interested questioners, I was soon telling my story and enjoying myself. Not having said a word to anyone for some days, I could hear myself jabbering away like a demented magpie at times but it was fun. This was definitely preferable to walking.

The *Abengane* (translated from Sindebele, it meant 'All Friends Together') belonged to a group of Bulawayo businessmen and this was their annual outing. There were thirteen of them on board and the average age was sixty-five, but they were a great deal of fun and I mentally christened them 'the Houseboat Hooligans.' Language on the boat was totally profane and I wondered at times whether they were all part of the same family or related in some way. Everyone was called – being a good Catholic boy, I can't put it here but it is a very basic four letter word – with first names varying between 'Stupid' and 'Doc' which apparently stood for 'Deaf Old ****.' Banter and badinage were freely exchanged and indeed they did seem to be all friends together.

One of the guests was Ian Macintosh, the former South African rugby coach, so rugby was a major topic of conversation over lunch and for much of the day. The man who had asked me whether I was lost was called Hilton and he roared with laughter when I remonstrated with him.

"You looked so funny," he told me. "There we were having a fine old time when suddenly this skinny apparition appears from the rocks and says 'good morning.' To be honest, we didn't know whether you were white, black or even human to start with."

That shook me a little. I had always consoled myself with the thought that I was unlikely to be shot as a poacher because of my white skin, but if I looked like a black man, parks or army patrols would be perfectly justified in shooting first and asking questions later. Poachers were fair game throughout Zimbabwe.

Shortly after lunch, I was approached by the leader of the party, a man I had been introduced to as Don. He asked what I intended to do when they ferried me across the river.

"Find a shady tree and camp," was my reply. "I'll need to sleep off the beer for a start and I am not in any particular hurry."

"Why not make your camp here with us," he suggested and I could feel my eyes light up. "You will be far more comfortable and a fishing party can take you across at first light tomorrow."

That was definitely an offer I could not refuse and I stumbled my thanks for his generosity.

Don merely smiled.

"It isn't just because we are hospitable like all Zimbabweans," he told me gently. "We are Matabele and so we appreciate courage and physical endeavour. We will give you every bit of help we can, I can promise you that."

He sounded fiercely proud of being Matabele and it is something I have so often encountered among residents of that big, wild, hospitable province. Black or white, they all look upon themselves as something special and totally different to people from other parts of Zimbabwe.

So it was that I enjoyed a lovely relaxing afternoon. My somewhat ravaged stomach couldn't take any more beer but somebody placed a glass full of cane spirit and mango juice in front of me and that was delicious. I had been craving sweetness for weeks and with the extra alcoholic bite, I couldn't remember when I had enjoyed a drink so much.

The evening was as enjoyable as had been the afternoon. Most of the chaps had been out fishing before sunset but their catches hadn't amounted to much and once they returned and showered, the party really began. Dinner was served with napkins and a proper tablecloth, the fare being rare roast beef, washed down with gallons of delicious red wine. After my meals in a mug, I somewhat anxiously wondered just how my stomach would cope, but it didn't seem worth worrying about so I tucked in with a will, even availing myself of an ample helping of peaches and ice cream for dessert. It was absolute bliss!

At one stage Hilton asked how I felt about God when I am alone in the wilds. Meryl Taylor had asked a similar question and it was a difficult one to answer. Every day I was surrounded by incredible natural beauty and this had to have been created by someone – God-like or otherwise – with excellent taste. There was also the fact that during the weeks I had been walking, I had been so incredibly lucky – the river crossings, that life-saving pool near the Sengwa, my brushes with park personnel, the close encounters with lions – and it made me feel that someone or something had to be keeping a benevolent eye on my welfare. I have always been a pretty resourceful man, but I didn't think even I could have survived those long, wearying weeks without a little bit of divine protection.

All the same, the mumbo jumbo of ordinary religion still left me cold and Hilton smiled when I told him so. I felt that while in the bush, I was in my own cathedral and it was far more uplifting, spiritual and spectacular than anything built by mankind. It probably had something to do with the feeling of being free to make up my own mind rather than have the rules and regulations of various churches forced upon me. I suppose that rebellion against organised religion came from my being educated by the Jesuits.

Hilton was obviously interested but once again, I didn't express myself very well and I could see that I left him a little puzzled as to what I really felt. I am not sure I could have explained it adequately, even to myself.

I was given a proper mattress to sleep on in *Abengane* and that was luxury indeed. No worries about rocks under my sheets, rain, lions or anything else. It was wonderful to close my eyes and just sleep. I had almost forgotten the feeling.

It was after six and the sun was well up when my benefactors took me across the river next morning. I waved my farewells as we pulled away from *Abengane* and a chorus of 'good lucks' echoed across the wide Ruzi. I prayed that they couldn't be heard from the parks camp, which was only a short distance away.

Before leaving the houseboat, Hilton had applied some strong glue to my flapping boot sole and Fred Jocks who ran the catering on *Abengane* offered me the run of their pantry.

"Take what you need," he said generously but proud, stubborn fool that I am, I merely helped myself to eight teabags and a little sugar. It was only afterward that I wondered why I hadn't taken a few potatoes and tomatoes – even a bit of steak. Oh well, it was back to the meals in a mug for me.

We were soon across the river and as the fishing boat grounded against a steep rocky bank, I climbed ashore and pulled my pack into its accustomed position. Off we went again but my afternoon and evening of convivial company and so much enjoyment had definitely done me good. I felt considerably stronger than usual as I hauled myself up the slope. The exercise was made more difficult by having a large, cold-beef sandwich clamped in one hand but I wasn't going to loosen my grip on that. It was a parting gift from my new friends on *Abengane* and I was going to enjoy it to the full.

"See you in Bulawayo," Paul Sheppard called after me. "Enjoy the rest of your walk and let us all have a copy of the book."

I covered a lot of kilometres that day and once again had to urge myself to slow down. There was no need for haste and even going at a far more gentle pace, I could not be more than three weeks away from Binga. I could afford to slow right down and enjoy myself more, but the thought of getting past park headquarters at Chete was worrying me and wild plans of how to do it kept going round and round in my mind.

CHAPTER TWELVE

(Park Headquarters)

While relaxing among the hooligans on *Abengane*, I had forgotten all about the festering sore on my left leg. I had a bandage strapped around it and after a blissfully hot shower had applied more antiseptic cream but it was only when I was walking again that the pain returned and eventually I was forced to stop for an inspection of the wound.

It looked pretty awful. The original graze had widened and seemed to cover a much larger area than it had before. Yellow pus had pooled deep inside my leg and the skin was swollen and hot to the touch. What worried me was a collection of red lines spreading out from the wound. I had to do something drastic or serious infection would set in and I would be in real trouble.

Before leaving England, my lovely Welsh dentist, Sue Browse had given me a course of anti biotics to take if my teeth started playing up. I wondered whether they would cure infection in my leg as well. It seemed worth the risk so carefully bathing the wound, I popped the first of my anti biotic tablets into my mouth and carried on walking.

I tried using a stout stick to help me along, but the terrain was rough and rocky so the stick proved more trouble than it was worth. My forward progress slowed dramatically with the pain but I decided that was probably a good thing. I had been urging myself to slow down for weeks.

The further west I travelled, the longer and wider the beaches became. They were truly magnificent in their lonely beauty but I felt terribly exposed when I was out on the sand, so took to walking well inside the tree line, even though this made for far more uncomfortable movement. Loose branches whipped at my exposed skin and when one slapped my leg right on top of the infected wound, I yelled in pain and spent a few minutes rolling around on the ground while tears streamed down my cheeks. It was a little pathetic really and suddenly realising what a spectacle I was making of myself – even though there was nobody to see – I made a serious effort to keep on walking.

I still enjoyed my evening sojourns beside the water, but I felt more secure once the day was done and shadows rolled across the landscape. Sitting perfectly still amid the lakeside rocks, I was unlikely to be spotted except by the keenest of eyes, whereas when I was staggering along through the sand, I was probably visible from many kilometres away. As always the sunsets were magnificent. After one particularly colourful display of Nature's talents, I hurried back to my little camp and wrote the following words in my journal by the light of my torch.

'*I have just spent the most wonderfully relaxing three quarters of an hour, totally naked and completely visible for kilometres in every direction. I didn't care. There was a glorious sense of peace about the world with the only sounds being the gentle lap of water and the distant calling of a solitary dove. I watched swallows skimming frantically across the sand and a lone cormorant flying only millimetres above the surface of the water, going I don't know where. It was all utterly tranquil and so damned good for the soul.'*

It was too and brought me back down to earth after even the most traumatic of days. In a masochistic sort of way, I was enjoying myself again.

⁓

Guinea fowl were making ever more of a nuisance of themselves during this section of the trip. I don't know whether the same flock was following me down the shoreline or whether it was different birds, but they went against all the rules of avian society by going to bed late at night. I spent many a restless evening, rolled in my blanket and trying to sleep while the guineas chuntered and grumbled from nearby trees. To add to my scratchy-eyed irritability in the mornings, they would wander past and sometimes through my camp at first light, still chuntering and grumbling.

Many was the time I thought fondly back to guinea bird stew, enjoyed in the past. Red wine, mushrooms and thick brown gravy, the whole served with rice or mashed potato – I could almost taste the memories. Foolish man that I was. I was still finding it difficult to kill mosquitoes or horse flies so how on earth I would manage to do in a guinea fowl, I didn't know. The silly creatures were safe enough from me and doubtless knew it. There were plenty of other wild life about on this remote section of shoreline too. I saw impala, kudu, waterbuck, buffalo and a lot of baboon, although the buffalo were very wary and skittish, not allowing me close when I tried to take pictures. This was heavy hunting area so I suppose they associated mankind with guns, noise and death. It was all somewhat disheartening.

I was sitting quietly under a tree one afternoon when I was approached by a wandering tortoise. He or she was the size of a small bucket so must have been quite old, although it obviously had no idea what I was and marched up to me, peering intently into my face. Very weird behaviour from a wild creature but we had a lengthy – if somewhat one-sided – conversation. Obviously deciding I was harmless, the tortoise moved off a few paces and started stripping bark from a tree trunk and struggling to digest it. Ignoring my smile of pure contentment at the moment, the strange little creature eventually shuffled off into the undergrowth and I carried on walking in the opposite direction. It had been a lovely little encounter and I felt infinitely cheered. I knew I was a lucky man to be allowed so close a communion with a truly wild creature.

Mankind and wild life have lost touch with each other over the past couple of centuries but that tortoise proved that there is still trust among wild animals, in spite of our very poor record as human beings. I have always been a cynical soul, but my encounter with a tortoise on the remote Chete shoreline made me feel that there is still hope for the wild places of Africa.

On another occasion, I came across a road. It was wide and well defined but obviously hadn't been used for a long time so I followed it, heading roughly in the direction I thought I wanted.

Roads in the bush are fine provided one knows where they come from and where they are going but with this one, I had no clue as to either. It was easy going though so I kept on until the road suddenly stopped at a T junction. That put me into a quandary. Which branch should I take and where would it lead me. In the end, I tried both directions, giving up on each when I came to fallen trees across the road itself. Taking that as a sign from above, I remembered my compass, took a westerly bearing and moved back into the bush.

It was a relief to get off that road, even though it had provided relatively easy walking. I would have heard a vehicle approaching from a long way off but had a foot patrol been coming along the road in the opposite direction, we might well have been face to face before I realised that they were about. I was getting ever closer to park headquarters at Chete, so patrols might well prove to be more frequent. The problem of getting around the Chete camp was beginning to seriously worry me. I could not afford to be seen and arrested now. I was over three quarters of the way through my walk and did not want to waste all that and have to start again.

My main problem was that I did not know or couldn't remember the lay out of the camp. I knew that the warden's house and a couple of others were perched on the edge of the cliff at Chete Gorge, but how much of the camp was inland and how far inland did it go? I had no way of knowing and the worries mounted in my mind, banishing my normal thought processes and leading me to do foolish things.

One such foolish thing was to lose my back pack. I had walked well for some hours on that particular morning, daring to think that perhaps the anti biotics were taking effect and my leg was not quite so painful. At one stage, I was well inland and walking along a narrow ridge when I spotted a solitary footprint heading in the same direction as myself. It wasn't a boot print, so was unlikely to belong to anyone official. Parks personnel have regular boot issues but this one looked like a rough sandal, possibly one of those known as *manyatellas* and made from pieces of motor car tire. That almost certainly meant that I was sharing what looked like completely empty countryside with a poacher and I walked very carefully after that.

There were no other signs of the unknown interloper however and as it was getting hot, I looked around for somewhere to rest up for a few hours. The first thing I needed was water, so dropping my pack in the sparse shade of a bent mopani tree, I followed a winding path down an almost vertical cliff to the lake far below.

Half way down I came across a large and leafy tree that had flat ground at its foot and offered ample shade, so turned around and climbed up again for my pack.

It wasn't there and my mind flashed back to that solitary foot print. Could I have been followed and thereby allowed myself to be robbed of all my kit and equipment? It was a terrifying thought. I looked around somewhat wildly but the creaking landscape merely looked emptily back at me.

I had checked the shape of the relevant mopani before leaving the pack but suddenly, I was surrounded by similarly bent trees and the spaces between them were liberally strewn with bulky black rocks that might easily have been taken for bulky back packs, even though my pack was blue.

Telling myself not to panic, I began to search as systematically as possible. My mouth was dry with fear as I quartered the ground, checking ever tree and every rock but I still couldn't see that damned pack. Round and round, up and down I went, my heart hammering ever faster and the cold sweat of panic running down my sides. Once, twice, three times I retraced my steps and tracked myself into the flat area but the tracks always petered out among the rocks.

Thinking about Hilton's comments on God in the bush, I prayed aloud to Him, to Saint Anthony, to my late mother and to my many dead friends. I included in my prayers all those folk I knew who had died, with special mention of my old friend Edridge, who I felt would be laughing himself silly at my incompetence. Edridge and I had laughed in the bush together on many occasions and thought of him made me smile a little, but the situation was extremely serious. Without that pack I was lost. Food, camera, medicines, spare clothing – all were in there and I would be left with one water bottle, my knife and my leatherman. It would really become a survival exercise.

Sitting down on a rock, I lit my pipe in an effort to clear my mind and relax a little. What else could I do? I had quartered the area, backtracked and followed my own spoor, yet still that big blue pack would not be found. I always had disliked the bloody thing.

Deciding that I was so hot and sweaty that my post-poned water resupply had to be the next item on the agenda, I went back down the cliff. Half way down I had an idea. If I found the tree that had originally looked so inviting, I could back track from there and perhaps find the pack that way. The only problem was that three or four big mopanis nestled on the cliff, so which one was it? One looked familiar and I stood looking at it for a while. Was it the one?

Fifteen meters along the cliff face, another big tree also looked familiar and with a sigh of utter despair, I turned around and there in front of me, nestling beneath a bent mopani tree was my back pack. I almost burst into tears, the relief was so enormous. One reason I hadn't spotted the pack beforehand was possibly because I had taken the black storm cover off the previous day and was looking for something blue, whereas when I left it beneath the tree, it had fallen with the black underside of the pack uppermost and there were only small traces of blue visible behind the shoulder straps. It had looked like just another bulky black rock.

It didn't matter – I had it back and my life was saved.

I am not sure how long I spent searching for that pack, but it was without doubt, the scariest incident on my entire trip. Lions I could cope with. Park patrols I could avoid – perhaps – but losing all my kit and equipment was a terrifying prospect.

Weight was continuing to fall away from my body at an alarming rate. I had been forced to make three extra buckle holes in my belt since leaving Kariba and even my watch strap needed regular adjusting to avoid it falling off my wrist. My hip bones became ever more prominent and it was probably as well that I did not have a mirror in which to see myself.

At one stage, I went to scratch at my backside and there was no backside there. It seemed to be all bone and I wondered how much more weight I could possibly lose. Yet in spite of my weight loss, my giddy spells and the deep, throbbing pain of my leg, I was still in relatively good shape and needed to be, as my journeys for water along that stretch invariably meant dizzying cliff descents to reach the lake. With containers full, I would then have to climb back up and I have never been much of a rock climber. I knew that every such descent entailed a huge risk of falling but I didn't seem to have much choice. I needed water and couldn't walk along the lake shore because it was far too precipitous. I would just have to learn how to be a mountaineer or put up with being thirsty.

The going was becoming ever more difficult. Rocks and ridges kept springing up before me, almost as though they were playing some sort of macabre game with my ever more fluttery nerves. They were interspersed with patches of thick green, clinging jess bush. Long thin branches, some of them wickedly thorned, formed an almost impenetrable barrier that I just had to force my way through, for much of the time crawling on my hands and knees.

Branches tore continuously at my skin and I would come out of the thick stuff, streaming blood. I carried a big handkerchief in each pocket and used one of them for mopping up the gore. By midday I could usually feel the dampness of the hankie through my shorts. It really was being overworked and as I didn't have the energy to wash anything at the end of my day, it was invariably hard and crusted the following morning. Three days without a wash and the hankie stank to high heaven. It was all rather unpleasant but I had gone past caring. I just wanted to get out of the forbidden area.

The bush was thickening up fast too. At one stage I came to a huge wall of greenery that I despaired of ever getting through. Fortunately I found a narrow game trail and managed to wriggle my way along that, but at times I was flat on my stomach and the pack would catch repeatedly on the branches above me. The weight of it drove me down into the ground and made forward movement a huge effort but eventually I came out on the other side of the obstacle, thereby saving myself a two kilometre detour. Looking somewhat disconsolately back at that tangled thicket, I wondered why I hadn't just walked around it in the first place. It would have taken half the time and avoided a great deal of discomfort.

The occasional 'roads' I found through the massed vegetation occurred where buffalo or elephant had forced their way through and I took advantage of them with much relief, even though I knew they would suddenly peter out and leave me disappointed. I followed a big old buffalo bull one morning but when he stopped and turned around a few meters ahead of me, I hurriedly backtracked and made a lengthy detour to get around him. I don't think he saw me but he was just too big to cope with and I didn't have the energy to run if he came at me.

All my camps along this stretch were perched on the top of almost vertical cliffs and the last one before Chete Headquarters was the most uncomfortable by a long way. I had little choice of location though. I needed to remain hidden for the day and the cliff top seemed the safest place. I would rather have been beside the water, but there wasn't likely to be much space down there and I would be vulnerable to stray crocodiles, as well as in full view of anyone passing in a boat. I had heard a land rover earlier that morning, so knew I had to be very close to comparative civilisation. It was the first vehicle I had heard in many weeks and I did not enjoy the experience. I felt somehow insulted that anyone should be using motorised transport in 'my' patch of bush.

I had been to Chete before. While rowing Hobo down the lake, I stopped off in the safari camp and had marvelled at the luck of any warden, sent to occupy that wonderful cliff-top house overlooking the gorge. What a dream posting it must have been. I had wandered a little through the bush around the camp and paid due homage at two tiny graves where a Trooper Albert Ernest Rice of the BSAP and an unknown companion had been buried way back on 23rd February 1900. At that time, Chete would have been even more remote than it was in the 1980s and I could only surmise what the trooper had been doing there and how he had met his death.

But that was all in the past. Chete was now very much enemy territory and somehow I had to bypass the camp or my walking trip was going to end in tears.

I had known I was close to the place but still received an awful shock when I walked out of a wide patch of mopani forest to find myself on the edge of a well used road. It was mid morning and there were buildings away to my right so I was fortunate not to be seen.

Diving back into the bush, I back-tracked and eventually scrambled into a patch of thick vegetation on the edge of the cliff. The water looked a long way below me but I knew that I would have to make that awfully steep descent at least once during the day ahead. Flies were out in force and I was hassled by mosquitoes even during the day. The sun was hot and I was worried, so the day passed very slowly and in a state of awful boredom and trepidation. I had to make a plan but I really didn't see how I would get past that camp.

I couldn't relax and on two occasions, I packed up my kit and started walking fretfully on, but I knew in my heart that was not the right thing to do so I wandered back again. Depression mounted and my leg throbbed with the beating of my heart. I had a terrible feeling that everything was about to blow up in my face but there seemed little I could do about it.

At one stage during that interminable afternoon, I heard a cock crowing nearby and that made me cross. How could they keep chickens in a national park? I couldn't help wondering what the fee-paying hunting clients would think. If it was me, I would have been extremely annoyed. These people paid for the bush experience damnit and chickens had no place in the bushveld hierarchy.

The sound of a big engine out on the lake brought me to my feet and I smiled when I saw *Abengane* moving majestically westward. It was a wry smile though. The blokes aboard would be comfortable, safe and taking ample advantage of their inboard bar. They would be well fed and enjoying each others' company while I huddled among rocks, weak, uncomfortable and vaguely frightened. It would take them less than three hours to reach Binga. It might yet take me three weeks. Waving wildly from a rock, (I don't think anyone saw me) I pondered on the injustice of it all then berated myself for being a silly old fool. I was walking from Kariba to Binga because I wanted to do it. Nobody had forced me into the venture and in truth I had enjoyed most of it so far. Although my few hours with the Houseboat Hooligans on their lovely craft had been great fun, I would soon have become bored and was definitely better off with my own company and the joys of the bush.

The only good thing about my enforced wait on that cliff top was that it gave my injuries a chance to ease a little. My left leg was still suppurating and very sore. Despite the anti biotics, the skin was very tight and hot, so it was probably as well that I gave it a little rest. The constant throbbing pain was making me irritable and unhappy but there was little I could do about it. I was on my own and if Sue Browse's tablets didn't do the trick, I was in serious trouble.

I could remember 'operating' on my own foot during my rowing trip and I certainly didn't want to repeat that experience. Even thinking about it brought the pain, desperation and resulting nausea flooding back, but I had little choice at the time. Following a snake bite, my foot swelled up like a rugby ball and went completely black. The pain was terrible and I was many miles from anywhere. All I could do was slash into the site of the bite with a razor blade, causing foul-smelling pus to fountain high into the air. Once that was done, the pain eased almost immediately and life gradually came back to normal. It was not a good memory though and I certainly didn't want to go through that again.

That day on the cliff top at Chete was one of the longest I could remember. Normally I was happy to rest in relative shade, enjoy a little poetry, watch birds and insects or be silently curious witness to a hundred bushveld dramas. This time I could only wallow in my own misery and long for the time to pass.

In between swipes at marauding insects, plans for the night went round and round in my head – a totally futile exercise as without knowing the lie of the land, I had no idea how best to approach the place. As I remembered Chete, it was a large camp with a number of office build-ings and houses to get past. I eventually decided that I would have to find my way through as I went along. I would make my way back to the road, sleep in the bush beside it and snivel through the camp while it was still dark. The moon was quite close to full, so there should be plenty of natural light to travel by.

Daylight was beginning to fade when I made my initial move. Emerging on the edge of the road I had seen earlier, I glanced briefly in both directions then sprinted as fast as I could to get into the bush on the other side. Even a gentle trot with a back pack aboard is not easy. My 'sprint' was more like a lumbering shuffle. I could hear a vehicle clattering along the road not too far away and eventually, I bedded down in a thicket of dense undergrowth very close to what was obviously staff quarters for the camp. I watched as a tractor drove in towing a trailer full of firewood and I listened to excited voices discussing the day that was ending. It all seemed very domestic and I couldn't help wishing I could have been with those cheerful workers rather than snivelling in the undergrowth and wondering how to avoid them.

A lone baboon walked slowly through my copse of trees and I prayed that he wouldn't panic when he saw me and alert the park personnel to the fact that there was a stranger in their midst. The *bobbo* was fifteen metres away when I first spotted him, but kept walking ever closer. He was feeding without much interest and even though he passed within five metres of where I lay, he did not appear to see me. I hadn't been able to bathe for a few days so supposed that I smelled bad and thus blended in with the bushveld around me.

Night fell with characteristic suddenness and I readied myself for a few hours sleep. My bed was thick dry grass and I had two small trees cutting me off from the staff quarters but with the advent of darkness, I felt infinitely more comfortable. There was no chance of anyone wandering into my little patch of bush before first light the following morning. Night walking through places like Chete was something reserved for the very foolish or suicidally insane.

As if to reinforce that thought, a hyena went through his terrifying musical repertoire less than half a kilometre from where I lay and I huddled deeper into my blanket. Very necessary as cleaners up of the wild places, hyena have a fearsome reputation for biting chunks out of sleepers in the wild. They are not nice animals to have around at the best of time so I hoped this one would keep well away.

Through the trees, I could see the flickering light of a fire and the smell of roasting meat brought saliva flooding through my mouth. I hadn't eaten since midday and that had only been yet another meal in a mug. I was decidedly hungry and couldn't even brew myself some tea as it would give my position away. I washed my mouth out with water and fell asleep.

My plan had been to rise about midnight and take advantage of the wee small hours for my walk through Chete, but I slept well and it was almost four when I hauled myself hurriedly out of bed. The moon had disappeared behind thick, scudding clouds but there was an eerie half light that was probably far more suitable for my plans than bright moonlight would have been.

It took me a few minutes to pack up my camp then with a fervent prayer to whoever was listening, I moved out from my shelter and walked south westward through lines of small, brick-built houses on either side of the road. No lights were on, but music blared from one of the houses and I stopped in deeper shadow to figure it out.

I had heard the music earlier on and there was no sign of life in the relevant house so I hoped that the occupant had merely fallen asleep before switching his radio off. Unfortunately the road went directly past his open front door so moving on was taking a huge risk. If the house occupant was awake, he only had to glance out of his window or the front door to see my heavily laden form tottering past. Perhaps he would think I was a *tokoloshe*– an evil spirit of the night. To heighten that effect should I be challenged, I carried my torch in one hand so that I could shine it up through the tangled mess of my beard and perhaps emit some ghostly noises.

Smiling at the thought, I took a deep breath and walked past the musical house just as quickly and as silently as I could.

Nothing happened. I held my breath against the challenge that was sure to come from the darkness, but the scouts and rangers who occupied those little houses slept on, unaware of my presence among them. Moments later, I passed a small store set back from the road and then I was past the camp and heading away into the darkness, my heart thudding anxiously in my chest.

My original intention had been to leave the road and strike west through the bush, but I seemed to be going in roughly the correct direction and the road surface made for considerably easier walking, particularly in that half light.

A big worry was the fact that my boots were leaving an easily discernible trail in the soft, dusty road surface. I might be able to spread alarm and consternation as a *tokoloshe* in the darkness, but no self respecting spirit – whether evil or otherwise – would be walking along in hefty size nines. There was little I could do about it though as it was infinitely safer to stick to the road until it was light enough to see where I was going.

As always with night walking in wild places, it was not easy on the nerves. The strangled scream of a bush baby almost had me wetting my pants at one stage and as the night began to lighten in preparation for the day ahead, I was forced to stand in the shelter of a tree while a herd of buffalo crossed the road in front of me. There must have been two hundred and fifty of the huge animals and dust billowed in their wake. Most of them were cows and they were not in any hurry so my own need to push on was of secondary importance.

A large black mamba was another local resident to cross the road ahead of me and I thanked my lucky stars that we hadn't met somewhat earlier. He was a good six feet or so in length but it would not have been difficult to step on him in the darkness and that would have been fairly disastrous. Mambas are the most dangerous snakes in Southern Africa and without immediate treatment, a bad bite is invariably fatal. I waved the big snake off into the shadows and he ignored me.

The road I was following seemed to wind and twist alarmingly but the general direction appeared to be west so I stayed on it for a couple of hours. With the advent of daylight, I took to dragging a leafy branch behind me in an effort to obliterate my spoor but I don't think it was much help.

As the sun rose and the air warmed up, I seemed to be in my 'just one more kilometre' mood and I walked on and on, using my compass whenever the road swung and panicking when I found myself going in the wrong direction. It was awfully wearying but I knew I had to get as far away from Chete as I possibly could before it became too hot to walk.

The sun was high in the sky when I came to a harbour of sorts where I was able to fill my water bottle, but there were buildings overlooking the bay so I moved hurriedly on. I passed the entrance to Chete hunting camp and marvelled at the amount of bones left lying beside the road. Did these people bring the carcasses of the animals they had shot back to camp for butchering, I wondered. I would have thought it was easier to sort them out in the places where they fell. I supposed that there must be some reason behind the bones, but it seemed terribly sad to see all those elephant skulls.

Half way through the morning, I recognised a side road that I had passed previously. Makeshift targets were pinned to trees where hunters obviously sighted their rifles before pitting their wits against the animals. In spite of using my compass, I had walked in a wide circle but the little road was heading due west so although I had ignored it earlier, I turned down it hoping that it would lead me to the lake.

I was dying for coffee at that stage but couldn't afford to rest until I was well away from Chete. Besides, I was still worrying about water. It was silly really because my containers were three quarters full and I knew I was never far from the lake, but I was still almost paranoid whenever I couldn't see that big blue puddle.

There was quite a lot of thunder rumbling about and the clouds were thick and heavy, so I prayed for rain to sweep through the area and cool everything down. I didn't mind getting wet. In fact, I would have welcomed it as the day was already hot and steamy. Besides the rain would also wash away my tracks. I wasn't out of trouble, even with park headquarters behind me. I was still at least three days away from the Sengwe, my last major river and the western edge of the prohibited area. Until I had that behind me, it behoved me to be careful and remain alert.

I was walking quietly and a little to my surprise, came upon a massive buffalo bull grazing beside the road. He could not have been more than two kilometres from the hunting camp and great sweeping horns must surely have made him a wonderful trophy but he seemed completely unconcerned. There was a deep layer of fat on his haunches and his skin gleamed shiny black in the sunlight. This was a buffalo in the peak of condition and easing the pack from my shoulders, I left it under a tree and moved closer to the bull for a photograph. His back was to me and the wind was in my favour, so it was an easy approach. Ten metres from that huge rump, I carefully raised the camera to my eye and all hell broke loose.

With an angry bellow, two other bulls burst out of the bush behind me, their heads down and their legs pumping in panic. Without even thinking about it, I hurled myself to one side and one of the newcomers thundered past, almost within touching distance. Had I remained where I was, he would have flattened me. Seconds later, the air was full of dust and all three behemoths were out of sight but it had been a scary moment, caused entirely by my own carelessness. It was in a very thoughtful frame of mind, that I moved away from the road and brewed myself a cup of very strong coffee.

I had done it. I was through Chete and even though I was still in the forbidden area and would be for some days yet, I felt a vast sense of relief.

To add to my joys, I had no sooner reached the lake shore once more when the rain came down in sheets, soaking me to the skin, but cooling everything down and hopefully washing away many of the footprints I had left behind me that morning.

I was also away from those horribly rugged cliffs and ridges, the countryside ahead of me providing considerably easier walking although it was still very rocky. With Chete and those awful doubts behind me, I was sure I could cope with the next stretch, even though my leg still ached abominably. Limping along a wide, sandy beach in driving rain, I felt extremely pleased with myself and wondered if at last my troubles were over.

Once again, I had been incredibly lucky and it was reassuring to know that Lemon's Luck was still running true to form. I could so easily have been caught or even shot as a thief when creeping through the buildings of Chete and could just as easily have been run down by the buffalo bulls later on. Was that divine providence I wondered or was it just the blind luck that accompanies so much foolishness in this world. I didn't know but felt pretty good about it all.

That feeling lessened slightly in mid afternoon. I was following a narrow, winding path through a rocky area when I came across a shoulder blade with scraps of meat still attached to the bone. Something large had been feeding very recently and I certainly wasn't out of the woods yet.

CHAPTER THIRTEEN

(Birthday in the Bush)

It was 6th December and my birthday. I was sixty two years old and feeling closer to a hundred. I had promised myself an easy day to celebrate the occasion and even allowed myself to sleep in late, enjoying the unexpected delights of watching the dawn from my blanket and revelling in the morning chorus of birds and insects. Ground hornbills started it off with their booming calls, a little like the tympany of distant drums. Bulbuls, doves and drongoes kept the sing song going and I listened to them over sweet tea before starting to walk well after six.

I had deliberately chosen my camp beside a long, gentle headland that offered plenty of open forest to walk through and as I strolled through the trees, my mind was churning. It was a big day for me but would anyone else care that it was my birthday? Would anyone even remember? It was Wednesday and that had always been my night with the 'saga louts' in my local pub in far off Gloucestershire. I fondly imagined Lace going up to the Kings Head and telling the other old codgers that it was my birthday so that they could drink a toast to my health and welfare. I would be thought about and remembered, the prospect bringing a smile to my face.

Reality set in with the weariness in my legs and shoulders. Of course she wouldn't go to the pub and nobody would even think of me while they sipped their beer in England. My children might passingly remember the day and Deborah would probably mention it to her own offspring, but even that seemed increasingly unlikely. I was alone in a foreign world and nobody cared.

Feeling ever more despondent, I walked on for nearly an hour before emerging from the trees to find that after weeks and weeks of keeping the lake on my right, it had suddenly appeared on my left. Either I was travelling in entirely the wrong direction or I was in Zambia – not where I wanted to be at all.

I hadn't crossed any water so it couldn't be Zambia, which meant that I had somehow managed to walk in a complete circle and was back close to where I had started out that morning. A quick look around the vista ahead of me soon confirmed this and I wasn't sure whether to laugh or cry. Across the bay in front of me, I could see an abandoned safari camp where I had stopped for a meal the previous day and it wasn't difficult to spot the place where I had camped. The lake wasn't in the wrong place - I was and I felt a fool.

I had learned another lesson though. I might be on the last stage of my journey, but I still needed to walk with total concentration. In my reverie I could so easily have made far more serious mistakes than merely going back on myself. Yet again I had been extremely fortunate not to find myself in further trouble.

After that, I really did concentrate although I didn't cover a great deal of distance that day. My leg hurt and I was glad to find a shady tree half way through the morning. It was ideal for a day camp, so I set it all up, lay down and decided to chill out for a change. This was my birthday and I was not going to do anything serious. Besides, I had a treat to look forward to.

Shortly before leaving Britain, I had been discussing my plans with friends, Mark and Jane Spencer. They had asked what I would do for Christmas and I gleefully told them that I had a small tin of red salmon that was to be my dinner on the big day. A few days later, Mark and Jane presented me with a sealed packet of pink salmon, bought from a local supermarket.

"It should keep for a long time," Jane told me sweetly. "You can eat it on some other auspicious occasion."

Now the auspicious occasion had arrived and I was so looking forward to enjoying my treat. No meals in a mug for me on my birthday. I was going to eat proper food for once.

I wandered out for a gentle stroll that afternoon, enjoying the sensation of not carrying a pack and revelling in the strength that my body had developed over the preceding weeks. I might be skinny but I was strong and I was certainly fit. My leg was still pretty nasty but provided nothing else went wrong, I could surely get through this last stretch to Binga. After all, I had already covered in excess of seven hundred kilometres and that was a worthy achievement for anyone. Now I was almost there and I was determined to succeed.

For much of that afternoon stroll, I had an irate dog baboon creating merry hell a little way behind me. He probably didn't know what I was and was merely making sure I knew my place in the bushveld hierarchy. He was the local lord of the manor and I was merely an interloper. His family sat comfortably on rocks behind him, looking for all the world like spectators at a major sporting fixture. I couldn't help comparing them with football fans when I took their collective photograph and the big fellow looked vaguely hurt at my explosion of slightly hysterical laughter.

I also spotted two klipspringer tripping among the rocks and that was nice. These little antelope are becoming ever rarer throughout Africa and in hungry Zimbabwe, their numbers are going down at an alarming rate. These two stood stock still on scenting me and for a long moment, we looked at each other across the rocks. Then with a gusty snort from the larger buck, they were away, their tiny hooves picking their way unerringly out of trouble. Any animal larger or less surefooted than the klipspringer would have broken all four legs running through that sort of terrain.

A tawny eagle watched me curiously from his perch on some large rocks and throughout my walk the local bird life serenaded me with their calls. They seemed more vociferous than usual and I wondered whether they knew it was my birthday. I could only smile and giggle inwardly at the ridiculous thought.

Throughout the day I had been putting off my meal, enjoying the excited anticipation of eating something that was not a meal in a mug. Every time I thought ahead to the forthcoming feast, my mouth watered and my stomach growled in painful frustration. Oh but I was looking forward to that salmon.

When I removed it from the depths of my pack, the packet seemed heftily reassuring. This was going to be a real treat and just had to do me good. Prolonging the moment of opening for as long as I could, I wriggled in delicious anticipation until a few words printed on the packet seemed to jump out at me.

'Keep in a cool place.'

My heart sank into my boots. Had I seen those words before setting out, I would have left the salmon behind. I had been walking in temperatures hovering around the middle forties celsius so even though it had been sheltered in my pack and out of the direct rays of the sun, that salmon had been subjected to a great deal of heat. Surely it could not have survived.

Using the scissor section of my leatherman to open the packet, I sniffed gingerly at the contents, my heart fluttering with mounting nervousness. It all smelled ok. Placing a tiny sliver of the pink flesh on the end of my finger, I touched it with the tip of my tongue. The last thing I wanted was to go down with food poisoning out there, all because I had eaten dodgy fish.

The salmon tasted okay too so with a final mutter of 'to hell with it' to myself, I put it all out on my plate and wolfed it down. I had long since run out of salt and there were no condiments or chutneys to make my birthday dinner any more palatable but boy, was it delicious!

A few minutes later and it was all gone, leaving me replete and ready for the next stage of my birthday treat. The sun was beginning to plunge downward to the west and taking my medicinal hip flask and my tin mug, I wandered down to the waters edge for my evening pipe.

I couldn't remember what brand of whisky I had put into that hip flask but it was a single malt and it tasted good, even with lake water - particularly with lake water perhaps. I savoured the first couple of sips then caution and good manners deserted me, so down it all went. Refilling the mug, I raised it in a silent toast to 'dreams' and was a little more circumspect with my second drink. It was truly delicious and I mentally thanked Jane and Mark for helping to make my birthday a memorable one.

It was about to get better. The sun seemed to sizzle as it touched the western rim of the lake and moments later, it had gone, leaving jagged spirals of raw colour splashed haphazardly across the sky. I breathed it all in, my aesthetic appreciation undoubtedly helped by the grog. This was surely the life.

Walking peacefully back to my camp in the trees, I paused to listen as the hoarse, sawing rasp of a leopard split open the evening air from not very far away. The big cat was merely making his presence known and I smiled at the thought. Some hapless little creature would die tonight but at least it wouldn't be me. I would be safe and snug in my bushveld bedroom and the dramas of Africa would pass me by.

I hoped they would at any rate.

A tiny skops owl trilled a greeting as I got into the trees and then I heard my favourite bush sound from further down the lake. Elephants were on their way. Grinning all over my face, I peeped out from my cover then sat down with my back against a tree and the blanket slung across my knees. This was surely going to be a fitting end to a lovely day.

There were seven of them, led by a massively built matriarch. She walked ahead while directly behind her came two younger females, both adult, walking side by side and showing no concern for the world about them. Fourth in line was a young bull, perhaps fourteen years old and on the verge of puberty and subsequent banishment from the herd. Despite his youth, this fellow carried a pair of very thick tusks and I sadly reflected that he would be lucky to live into old age in a hunting area. Behind him was another female, young but if she wasn't a mother already, she soon would be. At the rear of the little family group, two very young calves sported and played in the gloom. Whereas the adults walked sedately along the sand, these two mites preferred paddling, chasing after each other and squealing in mock disgust when they were wet. One squirted water through its trunk at the other and then both were running out from the shoreline and into deeper water. Spray fountained up on either side of them and I could hear their shrill giggling. Like any youngsters in water, they were determined to enjoy themselves.

The smaller of the two seemed to stumble and went right under the water, which proved far too much for the other baby. With another shrill squeal, it also submerged and I laughed aloud as little round feet pointed vertically upward.

All this noisy horseplay soon became too tempting for the young male and he was followed into the water by the adult females until only the matriarch remained aloof from the fun. She stood, silently watching for a while then had me laughing again as with a tremendous shriek, she forgot her dignity, charged into the water and plunged in with the others.

I don't know whether the elephant family knew that they had an absorbed spectator to their hi jinks. Knowing elephant, I should think they probably did but they could also sense that I was harmless and so they let me watch and thereby made my day for me.

The night was very dark when they moved on at last and I climbed wearily into my bed. The night sky was at its spectacular best and it was while I was looking out for plunging meteorites or winking satellites that I fell fast asleep.

It had certainly been a memorable birthday.

CHAPTER FOURTEEN

(The Prettiest River in Africa)

It was such a silly accident and should have been avoided.

I was so relieved to have gone through Chete safely – even though I wasn't out of trouble yet – that I wasn't paying enough attention to where I was going. I was still in the prohibited area and would be for a few days to come, but that Chete camp had been worrying me and eating into my spirits. With it all safely behind me, I really felt that at last I had broken the back of my journey. In front of me I still had the Sengwe River to cross and that could prove a trial, but I knew that once I was on the other side, I would be well and truly on the home stretch into Binga.

For much of the morning I had been wondering how I would cope on reaching civilisation. I would have to worry about time, getting from A to B, regular meals (that was a nice thought) making conversation and even money – matters largely forgotten during the preceding weeks of wild solitude. Out in the bush I could stop or move on as and when I felt like it. In town, I would be dependant on the timetables of others. My life would no longer be entirely my own.

There was so much I was going to miss. The sunrises and my peaceful sunset vigils; the freedom and the space; lonely beaches and the magnificent vistas of lake, islands and lush green vegetation that surrounded me. I would miss the gentle light of evenings in the bush and the smell of cool, damp dust as night brightened into daylight. How difficult it was going to be to leave it all, to exchange it for roads, motor cars, tall buildings, radio masts and houses clustered together. In the bush there were no crowds – only me to make progress or not as the mood suited me. In town I would battle with frantically scurrying people and allow myself to be bullied in queues and other gatherings. The peaceful tranquillity of Tonga society would give way to the bustling anxieties of a more developed culture.

I would miss the bird noises too - the irritating chinkling of guinea fowl and the harsh 'gerrupwillyer' call of francolin at dawn. I would miss the shrieking cries of fish eagles and the frenzied chatter of the red-billed buffalo weavers, known among the Shona as *'sheka mfazi'* (chattering women) for their babbling chorus. I would miss the sound of hornbills clucking as they flew heavily past and the warbling song of the Heughlins Robin – one of the few Zimbabwean birds that actually sings rather than calls. Instead I would have the bland voices of television and radio announcers, the rumbling growl of traffic and the chatter of people who did not know what bush life was all about.

And of course I would miss the night sounds. The calling of lions at dusk, and the harsh rasp of hunting leopards – not to mention the maniacal howls of hyena and the yammering of jackals or tiny night apes. I would miss the vast glittering panoply of the night sky, the incredible silver slash of the milky way, vividly riven by plunging meteorites and brightly illuminated satellites winking their way across the heavens.

I would miss the wild life in general; the graceful antelope, the fearsome cats, comical warthogs and of course my beloved elephant. Those elephant that were so tolerant of my presence and accepted me into their company as long as I came in peace. I would miss the gentle hum of bush insects and knew that my advent into civilisation was going to be a difficult transition. The pain, the fear, the discomfort and the anxieties would soon be forgotten and only the memories would remain to remind me of yet another adventure completed.

As I walked, I pictured myself arriving in Binga. There would be my old friends Janice and Bushpig to greet me. Janice would give me a hug and Bush would shake me firmly by the hand. The last woman I had spent any time with had been Mrs Moyo from Bulawayo all those weeks previously and I wondered how I would react to Janice. Would I horrify her with my lack of culture or would she accept the fact that I had lived a very different life over the previous weeks? I would have to wash regularly and wear clean clothes. In fact, I would have to act like a civilised gentleman again rather than the restless savage I had so enjoyed becoming, albeit only temporarily. It was certainly going to prove a shock to my system, but I supposed I would cope.

I was thinking about food when I fell. Visions of a thick, rare steak with well-buttered mashed potato, mushrooms, green peas and a glass of fine red wine to wash it all down. I could see and taste it all but was brought painfully back to reality when I found myself down on my belly, the weight of the pack on my back driving my teeth ever harder into the gritty earth.

In my reverie, I had tripped over a small bush and because I was moving up a steep slope at the time, had fallen on my face. It was embarrassing rather than painful and cursing myself for an inattentive fool, I struggled to my feet. Readjusting my pack, I glanced down and saw what I had done to my leg.

There was an awful gaping wound in the muscular part of my right calf, just above the ankle. A thin branch had literally speared my leg and as I had fallen, the weight of my body had pushed the end of it through my flesh, opening up the limb as easily as I could have done with a scalpel. Sitting down on a rock, I tried to quell the sudden trembling of my hands. The cut was a bad one and I wasn't sure how to deal with it.

That the wound needed stitching was obvious. It was probably a centimetre deep and gaped almost as widely across the top. Five centimetres of flesh had been opened right up and I could see white layers of muscle on either side of the cut. Blood was starting to well up from the depths of the wound and although there was no pain at that stage, I knew it would come.

Having washed the gash as best I could, I took a long drink to steady my nerves. It was undoubtedly a time when the medicinal flask would have proved its worth but I didn't think of that. I had to stitch myself up. It was as simple as that. Although it was undoubtedly consider-ably better under the attack of the anti biotics, my left leg was still painful and I could not afford to have the right one in similar condition. I was close to the end of my jour-ney but there was still a considerable distance to cover and with two damaged legs, I was not going to make it.

I have always carried stitching material on my little adventures but never expected that I would need to use it. My kit consisted of individual stitches, complete with needles in separate sachets and I felt sick as I dug them out of the first aid kit. Sitting on a fallen tree trunk, I took a deep breath and set to work. Blood was flowing freely now and I had to wipe it away and pour water into the wound before inserting the point of a wickedly curved needle into my leg and pushing it right through a flap of skin on the edge of the cut.

It hurt and I wanted to yell but there didn't seem much point in that. Like most men, I like to make a fuss when I am hurt but on this occasion, I surprised myself by not making a sound. Civilised man has always marvelled at the stoic way tribesmen endure pain that would have the rest of us screaming for mercy, but after that horrible morning in Chete, I wonder if that dispassionate attitude is caused simply by the lack of an audience for any histrionics, the injured man might wish to put on. It is surprising what a difference is made by solitude and gritting my teeth, I held the wound together with two fingers and pushed the needle out through the other side.

I might not have been yelling but I wasn't very well. Sweat poured down my face and I wanted to vomit. It wasn't the pain that got to me, it was watching myself actually stitch up my own flesh. That was a horrible feeling and at one stage I wondered whether I would faint.

I didn't though and managed to tie off that initial stitch before beginning the process all over again. I had pushed the second needle into my leg and was on the point of pushing it out again when a thought occurred to me. A few days previously I had blessed Mark and Jane

Spencer for their birthday gift but now I remembered something else.

After handing me the packet of salmon, Jane had given me a packet of little white plasters.

"Butterfly stitches," was her comment when I asked what they were for. "You can use them instead of the real thing should you ever need them."

I had never heard of 'butterfly stitches,' so threw them in the bottom of my pack and immediately forgot them. Now I needed them and wondered where I had put them. They weren't in the first aid box so must still have been in the pack itself. With my usual forethought, that was some three or four metres from my makeshift operating theatre. Groaning through my teeth, I hobbled and hopped my way across to the pack, that damned needle still jutting from my calf with twine attached. It probably looked quite comical but I was not smiling. This was a painfully serious business and I was in real trouble if I couldn't do something about my leg.

It took me a while but I eventually found the packet of butterfly stitches. They turned out to be thin, centimetre-long strips of strongly adhesive plaster and having removed the needle from my flesh – that hurt too – I again held the edges of the wound together and pressed one of the butterflies in place across the line of the gash.

When I let go, I was a little surprised to find that it all held together quite adequately and I applied three more, carefully leaving the lowest bit of the wound unstitched for drainage. Still sweaty and trembling but not in so much pain, I wrapped a crepe bandage around my leg and surveyed the damage.

Both legs were now bandaged and the most recently injured one already had blood seeping through the crepe.

Would it all hold together? Would I hold together? I didn't know but there was no way that I was moving on for the moment, so I made a very basic camp beneath a tree, took three pain killers and tried to relax. It was not an easy exercise. My mind raced and seethed with worries as to how I would get any further, although I did not have any choice. I was still in the forbidden area, I was still totally alone and I still had a long way to go. Even if I was reduced to crawling, I needed to move on.

On more than one occasion I have heard the Sengwe described as the prettiest river in Africa, but it wasn't its beauty I was thinking about when I hobbled up the eastern bank a couple of days after my fall.

They had been long, painful days and forward progress had been very slow but I had eventually made it. This was my last major river, with only the smaller Musumu to come. Phil Varkevisser and the Houseboat Hooligans had told me that the Sengwe was a favourite weekend area for Binga folk so with luck I would find someone willing to ferry me across, but what would happen if I couldn't. This was only Wednesday so I might have quite a wait on my hands. If there were no boats in the river, would it be better to walk upstream and get distance behind me or should I merely camp up somewhere comfortable and wait. The questions went round and round in my mind. I had spent a few days up the Sengwe in Hobo and could remember being enthralled by the scenery and the wild life. What I couldn't remember was how far I had been able to get upstream and the prospect of a long walk terrified me.

The infection in my left leg had largely cleared up, leaving weird pink patches across my skin. It still ached but the pain was no longer as fierce as it had been. The right leg was more of a problem. Although I bathed it regularly and kept the bandage as clean as I could, the wound in my calf was still seeping blood and pus. There was no swelling around it, but the area was painful to the touch and made walking on any sort of uneven surface extremely uncomfortable. I could walk and that was a blessing, but if the Sengwe River went more than a few kilometres inland, I was going to find it very difficult to get across.

It was certainly beautiful. Coming out of the trees, I looked across a wide, vividly blue estuary, with heavily wooded slopes on either bank and a sense of peaceful tranquillity that would soothe any soul other than my own rather tormented one. This was Africa in the raw and I wished I could appreciate it more.

A lone kudu bull watched my approach with an air of extreme puzzlement and I held my breath, expecting him to run off in alarm as so many other Chete animals had done. This chap was different. Obviously deciding that I was harmless, he walked elegantly past me, huge spiral horns starkly outlined against the sky. Impala snorted nearby and a juvenile fish eagle preened somewhat bedraggled feathers in a dead tree near the water. It was a magnificent scene and I wished I could appreciate it more.

I was setting up my bivvy for shade and making a day camp among the trees when a power boat roared past. There were two men aboard and they were heading upstream so I felt a surge of relief that they would have to return and I could hail them when they did. I should not have been so complacent.

Half an hour later, they did return but this time in a large houseboat heading out of the river and I was snoozing when they hove into view. The boat must have been using a deeper channel close to the far bank and I didn't hear the sound of their engine until they were almost past me. By then, they were too far away for me to hail. I could probably have staggered out on to the river bank and waved something to attract attention, but I was too sore, too sleepy and too damned idle for that. I watched them go, feeling awfully alone.

Less than ten minutes later, another houseboat came by, also using the far channel and also heading downstream. It was larger than the previous craft and music blared across the water, so they would not have heard me even if I shouted. This time I felt a deep sense of abandonment as they chugged out into the lake. It was my own fault for not making more of an effort to attract attention but I blamed the holidaymakers for leaving me behind. It wasn't fair but that was the way I felt. Would there be any more houseboats upstream? Somehow I doubted it – not in mid week.

At a reasonable walking pace, I was only a few days from Binga and the end of my trip, but with two damaged legs, even a very slow walking pace was beyond me and if I was forced to make that inland detour, it might prove weeks rather than days. Lying in the shade of my bivvy, I had a sudden despairing feeling that I wasn't going to make it.

❧

There being nothing else to do, I decided on an inventory of my remaining kit and supplies, something I hadn't

238

done for a few weeks. It was another mistake as it did nothing for my already shaky self confidence.

My kit was in a mess. My shirt was torn in a number of places, as was my pack. One arm of my spectacles had fallen off and they had to be held on to my face with wire. The glue in my boot had long since lost its adhesive qualities and I did not have much cord left to hold the ruddy thing together. My sleeping mat was beginning to disintegrate and when I looked up at my bivvy, I could see blue sky through numerous little holes in the material. My mug had cracked and was also bound up with gardening wire, which I had only brought along with me to clean my pipe. Two weeks previously, my frying pan had fallen into the fire and burnt half of its handle off, leaving me a mere stub which meant continually burning my fingers when I cooked.

All in all, despite my loss of weight and the injuries to both legs, I had the feeling that I was in marginally better shape than my kit.

Nor was a check through my remaining supplies much of a confidence booster. I had enough meals in a mug left to keep me going for another three weeks, but I was down to four tea bags, a few spoonfuls of powdered milk and sugar mixture and one packet of fruit flakes. Tiny little black ants had invaded the milk and sugar mixture, but I didn't have the energy to pick them out individually and I was not going to throw the mixture away, so they had condemned themselves to a messy death. Smiling a trifle wryly to myself, I wondered whether they might even add infinitesimally to my protein intake and thereby make me feel a bit better.

My tobacco supply was almost exhausted and that was a worry. No matter what platitudes the anti smoking lobby might hit us with, when times were difficult my pipe was a definite comfort and I dreaded being without it. I figured that if I rationed myself to one half-filled pipe each morning and evening, I might just last out the week but there was nothing spare for times of extreme stress.

Another big worry was the fact that although I still had a day of my anti biotic course to run, I had used up my heavy pain-killers and was left with eight paracetemol tablets. If the pain in my leg didn't lessen soon, I would be struggling but there were no chemists within hundreds of kilometres, so those eight pills would have to last.

Despite the beauty of my surroundings and the fact that stars were out in force, I slept badly that night. One question went round and round in my brain and I just didn't know the answer. Should I walk on upstream and find a narrow spot to cross the river or should I wait where I was for a boat that might not appear for days.

It was all so frustrating and the following morning I peered in anguish at the opposite bank. It was a mere two hundred metres away and once across I would be almost within touching distance of my destination, but It might as well have been two hundred kilometres away because I had no chance whatsoever of getting across. Mad plans of swimming and pulling my pack along behind me went through my mind, but I knew they were impractical. Quite apart from my own lack of strength for such a swim and the fact that I would probably drown half way, the Sengwe – like all Kariba rivers – was a haven for crocodiles. I had seen a number of large specimens the previous day and one five metre monster had spent a good ten minutes only just off shore, his basilisk eyes fixed somewhat thoughtfully on me while he tried to work out whether I was edible or not.

I was and did not fancy providing an impromptu meal for any crocodile. Swimming across the river was not an option.

Leaving my pack behind, I tried wandering upstream to see what was what. The banks were steep and rocky, but there was a narrow beach area that I could hobble along without too much difficulty. I soon turned around though, supremely disgusted by the litter left along that shoreline by careless holidaymakers. There were cigarette packets, empty bottles, plastic packets and a couple of odd shoes, all in a two hundred metre stretch of river bank.

At one spot, I detoured inland to avoid a very rocky stretch of shoreline and on a ridge running parallel to the river I came across a veritable rubbish dump. There were empty packets, tins and the assorted detritus that could only have come from a houseboat. The crew had obviously come ashore to get rid of their rubbish instead of taking it back to their home base where it could be disposed of properly. It was horrible and I gave up my walk and moved back to camp, feeling angry and bitter about the damage human beings do to even the loveliest environment.

The euphoria I had felt after getting through Chete had entirely worn off by the time I got back to my makeshift camp. Half way there I stopped to turn a dung beetle over. The poor little fellow was on his back, waving his legs in the air and although one is not supposed to interfere with life in the bush, I had to help. I knew exactly how he felt.

With my leg feeling as though it was about to blow up, I struggled to pull myself upright after that act of kindness, but the dung beetle scuttled off in obvious delight. I had doubtless deprived something else of a meal but it was too bad. I decided that we little creatures of the bush had to stick together.

Bird life on the Sengwe was incredibly spectacular. Even from my bed, I spotted a variety of herons, egrets, cormorants and almost every water bird possible. Jacana scuttled along the river banks, the raptors were spectacular in their profusion and the good old emerald-spotted (the ornithologists call them 'green-spotted' nowadays but to me they remain 'emerald') doves kept trying to drive me scatty with their mournfully repetitive calling.

Guinea fowl chuntered away throughout the day, owls of many varieties serenaded the hours of darkness and I had francolin, ground hornbills and fish eagles to wake me up in the mornings. It really was an ornithologist's heaven.

In a big baobab tree forty metres from my camp, a raptor had built a wide, untidy nest among the upper branches. Around and below this lofty eyrie was a well-established weaver colony, the noise of its citizens' excited chattering keeping me company throughout the day. I couldn't help wondering which was the original inhabitant of the tree. Had the raptor – I spotted a magnificent gymnogene at the nest later – been there first or had he chosen the site as being the ideal 'des res' with it own built in food supply.

But I didn't need bird life, lovely though it was. I needed a boat and my eyes ached from searching the river mouth downstream for any sight of an incoming craft of any sort. I would have welcomed a poacher in a dug out canoe, but that wide estuary remained bleakly empty.

By my third afternoon beside the Sengwe I was feeling desperate and hugely depressed. The sun hammered down at me throughout the daylight hours and mosquitoes whined irritatingly around my head at night. I felt too tired and too despondent to set my net up, even though it would have kept the little brutes away. I didn't feel like eating, although in an effort to build myself up, I did try combining two different meals in a mug. The result was not a success. The 'meals' concerned were chicken and mushroom with leek and potato, but the glutinous sludge that came out of the pan stuck uninvitingly to my throat and the roof of my mouth. So much so that I eventually threw most of it into the river, thereby taking all meaning out of my little experiment.

I suppose the fish enjoyed it.

By early evening, I had made up my mind to walk on upstream the following day. To be truthful I was bored to tears, even though I was surrounded by spectacular scenery and bird life that was second to none. Although I could walk if I had to, my leg was too painful for me to enjoy a little gentle exploration and I no longer even had the energy to bath. I felt a sense of deep melancholy and wondered why on earth I had brought so much torment and suffering down on myself. I couldn't blame anyone else for my predicament. I had wanted to walk from Kariba to Binga. If I failed, it all came down to my own stupid carelessness.

Feeling totally disgusted with life and my own ineptitude, I decided that I was going to puff on my pipe, even if it meant depleting my stocks of tobacco even further. I needed something to cheer me up.

Something did. As I hauled myself painfully off my sleeping mat, I automatically glanced downstream and – marvel of marvels – there was a large boat in the mouth of the river. The breeze was blowing in the wrong quarter for me to hear the sound of its engine, but there could be no doubt – that craft was heading my way.

Scrambling upright, I heard myself yell with sheer exultation. I was saved. Suddenly all my troubles were forgotten. I had been totally naked when I got to my feet, but I dressed in the twinkling of an eye, had my bivvy down and folded in no time at all, then packed my kit untidily away just as quickly as I could.

There was really no need to hurry. The boat was still a good two kilometres from me and would not be moving very fast. My problem was a sense of mounting panic. Would they see me? Would they agree to take me across the river? Would they even report me to the authorities? After all, I was still in the Chete hunting area and should not have been there.

With all sorts of fears and anxieties running through my mind, I lugged my pack down to the edge of the water and waited with my heart hammering for the boat to arrive. The pain of my legs had been forgotten in my excitement and my pipe had been haphazardly stuffed into a pocket. Eventually deciding that I ought to look nonchalant to show what a hell of a fine fellow I was, I sat down on my pack and watched the big craft lumbering up the river.

The approaching craft was a large white houseboat called *Heart of Africa* and I didn't think they had seen me at first, as they seemed to be heading for the opposite bank. Desperate to be seen I yelled something across the river before remembering that the other two craft I had seen had also taken what was obviously a deep water channel on the other side. Firmly telling myself to be patient, I sat down again and continued my wait, my eyes never leaving that lovely, lovely houseboat. Eventually the bows swung around in a ponderous turn to port and the boat was moving directly toward me. They moored a little downstream from where I waited, so I wandered down to meet them, plastering my best smile across what were probably somewhat ravaged features.

Aboard the *Heart of Africa* was the Joubert family from Pretoria and if they were at all surprised to see a tattered stranger in that remote place, they gave no sign of it. As far as I could see, the family consisted of Dad, a very pretty Mum and two young children. Mum and the kids sat down to play some board game while Dad chatted to me across the rail. I was impatient to get across the river but there is no hurry in Africa so I listened to him talk.

"We drove all the way through to Bulawayo last night," Mr Joubert told me. "I reckon we are all tired. I have been looking forward to this for so long and now I reckon we will just switch off and enjoy the bush for a few days. We might even catch some fish although that isn't so important.

'Would you like a cold beer while you wait for the tender to come round?"

Hoping that nobody who knows me well would ever learn of my shameful fall from grace, I asked if he rather had any cold coca cola. I think it was probably the first time in my life that I have turned down a beer but that coke tasted absolutely divine.

"You had better have another one to take with you," Joubert called down and he tossed another beautifully chilled can down for me to catch, which I did with great delight. So much for my 'boozist' reputation, but what a pleasure and I hope those lovely Jouberts had a super holiday.

It was only after we had parted company that I realised that none of the Jouberts had expressed the slightest interest in my walk or where I had come from. Mrs had given me a lovely smile, as had the children while he had been far more concerned with telling me about his drive from Pretoria to Bulawayo. Perhaps South Africans were accustomed to meeting smelly strangers in their remoter beauty spots.

They were nice people though and so was the boat captain who plied me with questions as we chugged across the river.

"You would never have walked right up to a crossing point," he told me cheerfully and I could feel myself scowling inwardly. "The river is quite wide for at least twenty-three kilometres."

That was a comfort but twenty-three kays was hardly a problem for someone who had walked over seven hundred and fifty long kilometres during the preceding weeks. Not even when that someone had two sore legs. Nevertheless, I was pleased that I hadn't been forced to walk all that way.

"You should be able to make Binga in a few days from here," he confirmed my earlier thinking. "I would think that overland, you have about forty-seven kilometres to go."

What I love about the citizens of Africa is that they are always so precise. A Westerner would have put it down as 'about fifty,' but this little chap – I never did get his name – was determined to be exact.

For me it was wonderful news. I was almost there. Even with my legs in the state they were, I would cover that distance within a few days. Dreams of a successful end to my trip were once again running through my mind, even before the tender nudged its prow into the western bank of the Sengwe.

The following day, the somewhat ambivalent state of mind I had been enjoying over preceding weeks was amply reflected by a journal entry.

'*In the early hours, I was woken by lions roaring in the middle distance but they were across the river in Chete so perhaps they were bidding me a fond farewell. I just smiled and from then on I slept in little bursts and was up just after four. Even though I dawdled over coffee, packing and watching the sunrise, I was walking again well before five thirty. I have to slow down damnit! Now that I am so close to Binga, I do NOT want to get there*'

But I did want to get there. Arriving at Binga in one piece had been the focal point of my life for many months and now I was so terribly close. Surely nothing else could go wrong. My dream of being the first man in living memory to walk from Kariba to Binga was about to come true. My problem was that I didn't want to get there too soon. With the painful horrors of Sengwe behind me and the prospect of food, cold beer and comfort ahead of me, I was enjoying myself again.

CHAPTER FIFTEEN

(The Last Lap)

It was Sunday morning and after a slow start, the pain in my legs had lessened perceptibly. I was making good progress along a wide, sandy beach. As I was out of the prohibited area, I wasn't too worried about being seen and wherever possible, I walked on the firm wet sand at the waters edge. Hippo chortled at my passing from numerous little bays and I felt content with my lot.

The previous day had been particularly hot and uncomfortable. The humidity increased throughout the day until sweat streamed down my face and body. I felt as though I was in some gigantic oven and doubts about my ability to survive the walk surfaced yet again. I felt more debilitated than I had felt at any stage of the trip and even my bones seemed to ache with the discomfort. There wasn't a breath of wind to alleviate the heat and the lake itself remained glassily calm throughout the day.

I didn't see a single boat heading East either so if I had stayed where I was in the Sengwe for another couple of days, it would have been time entirely wasted. At that thought I breathed a silent vote of thanks to *Heart of Africa* and Whoever was 'up there' looking after me.

Dense swarms of mopani bees descended upon me during the afternoon and made my life increasingly miserable. It was far too hot to wear my face veil and I had found over the weeks that the only thing that would deter the little monsters was pipe smoke. My luck going the way it was, I had only a few pinches of tobacco left, so even that double solace was denied me.

Throughout the day I took advantage of a deep pool between some rocks to bathe and swim whenever the claustrophobic heat became too much for me. At one stage I wondered how residents of that area coped with such high temperatures then chided myself for a fool. The only residents of that area were wild and had four legs. They would all have been taking advantage of shade somewhere and sleeping the heat away until nightfall.

I was the only muggins around who remained active – fairly active at any rate. I managed to complete a technicolor repair job on my shirt, using up scraps of vari-coloured cottons that were all that remained in my sewing kit. I renewed the wire on my glasses, did a full laundry and sat for an hour or two with the lower half of my body in the water.

That particular endeavour lost some of its charm half way through the afternoon when a four metre crocodile drifted slowly past my pool, causing me to whip my legs up under me and leap on to dry land, ignoring an admonitory stab of pain from my injured leg. Crocs of that size are normally alone, but this one was followed moments later by an equally large one of his fellows and then yet another, possibly even larger than the first two. It was enough to put me off bathing for life.

After that I contented myself with showering from my water containers – not nearly as nice as a proper bath or sitting in the water, but infinitely less nerve wracking.

I had become a little blasé about wild life over the preceding weeks. I suppose it was because I was with them all the time but whereas I would have been very careful about the crocodile danger in any pool a few weeks earlier, I hadn't even thought about the brutes on this occasion. That could so easily have led to problems and I remembered the buffalo incident at Chete. I should have checked the area carefully before approaching that massive animal for a photograph. He wasn't an old beast so it was unlikely that he would have been on his own, yet I had been too complacent to look for his companions before moving forward with camera in hand. Those who survive any length of time in the African bush are those who take a lot of care and I gave myself a stern lecture on the subject.

It had rained for a while during the night, but I hadn't stirred from my bed. There were groups of stars still visible overhead so I didn't expect the shower to last long. It didn't and although it made life a little uncomfortable for half an hour or so, it certainly brought the humidity back down to a bearable level. I slept well once I had dried out and started off my day feeling quite chirpy. I had no idea where I was or how far I was from my destination but I knew I was almost there and that made all the difference.

The previous evening I had suffered my most embarrassing moment of the trip and had been heartily thankful that there was nobody around to witness my discomfort. I had been lying in bed, waiting for the stars to arrive when a movement to my left caught my eye. Turning my head slowly in that direction, I watched enthralled as a herd of impala moved up from the water where they had obviously been enjoying their collective sundowners. This was darkest Matabeleland where starvation was said to be endemic yet it appeared to be a large herd of very edible antelope – a very large herd.

Row after row after row of golden backs moved in serried ranks toward the tree line and sitting up slowly, I wondered exactly how many there were. It was many years since I had seen more than fifty impala in a herd but this group seemed considerably larger than that.

Curious but anxious not to startle them, I climbed carefully from my sheet bag, wedged my spectacles on to my face and stark naked though I was, commenced a slow approach to the unsuspecting impala. There still wasn't any discernible breeze so I knew they wouldn't catch my scent.

Thorns in the sand were a bit of a worry and I stopped twice to remove them from my feet. Each time I moved with infinite slowness, my eyes fixed on the still moving ranks of golden backs.

I don't know what made me realise what it was. Perhaps my eyes or my brain cleared suddenly from some sort of fog induced by the extreme humidity of the day. Perhaps I had fallen asleep and woken suddenly with my mind still lost in dreams. Whatever the case, I stopped in my tracks and burst into a roar of what had to be semi hysterical laughter.

Those weren't impala. I might have realised that herds of that size had long since disappeared into the dim and long forgotten past. What I was looking at was the lake itself. It moved up into a small inlet and those serried ranks of golden backs were actually tiny wavelets, tinted by what little light remained in the sky and lapping gently on to the shoreline.

I wandered back to bed, shaking my head at my own foolish imagination and thanking my lucky stars that I was entirely alone with nobody to see my shame. It wasn't until much later that I started to chuckle.

The tree was a monstrously large pod mahogany and even from a kilometre away I could see the wide patch of shade beneath its well covered branches. It would make the ideal spot to rest up for the day and I kept my eye upon it as I plodded up a wide sandy beach that was probably two kilometres long. I was no longer in any sort of a hurry and filled my mind with prospects of a cup of tea and perhaps a gentle nap, followed by a swim in what appeared to be a wide lagoon of very blue water. It all seemed a delightful prospect and I was really enjoying my day.

It was to get better. As I approached that forest giant, I tilted my head to one side in order to examine it better. Beneath it was a patch of vividly green grass, far too well tended to be ordinary bush grass. This lot was definitely a lawn and I wondered who on earth would be living out here. Metal piping on a bank to my left appeared deeply incongruous and then I saw the thatched rondavels and shelters of a typical safari camp.

For the second time in twenty odd years, I had arrived entirely accidentally at picturesque and very lovely Sijarira. On the first occasion, I was blown off course in my dinghy *Hobo* and had made the acquaintance of Mags and Leon Varley, together with Leon's right hand man who introduced himself only as Sitwala. They had taken me under their respective wings and I had enjoyed a pleasant few days in what had even then been an enchanted little camp. The place had belonged to the Forestry Department in those days and Leon had entertained big plans for its future. As I recognised where I was, I wondered how many of those plans he had been able to implement.

Since that first impromptu arrival of mine, Sijarira had been sold and was now part of a hunting empire belonging to and run by the Van Wyk family.

As I climbed a little hesitantly up some stone steps toward the camp buildings, I was greeted by two young men who introduced themselves as Ian and Stan.

"We wondered who or what you were," Ian told me cheerfully. "Stan spotted you about an hour ago as a tiny speck in the distance and we thought you were going to walk right past us like some sort of ancient mariner drifting around the world.

'Have some tea anyway."

That was an offer I couldn't refuse and shortly afterward, Pierre Van Wyk appeared with his wife Kim. I introduced myself and Kim looked closely at me.

"Are you Graeme's dad?" She enquired and I corrected her gently.

"Let's just say that Graeme is my son."

Everybody laughed but once again my younger son had broken the ice for me. It turned out that Kim and I had a number of acquaintances in common and had met before at a bush funeral for a mutual friend. We reminisced over more tea and then breakfast.

"You two obviously have a lot to catch up on," Pierre observed to me at one point. "Would you like to use one of the chalets tonight and sleep in a proper bed for a change?"

I would like and told him so, with the result that an hour or so later, I was showered and dressed in clean – if crumpled – clothing while mine was whisked away to be washed. Wandering around the camp, I was able to wallow in memories for once and I could feel the pain, the strains and the tension ebbing from my frame with the wide beaches, shady trees and chattering weaver colonies of lovely Sijarira.

Mind you, the easing of tension could have been due to enjoying the long forgotten pleasure of talking to a pretty girl.

My Sunday in Sij turned out to be a peaceful, relaxing day. I chilled out ever more as the hours passed and perhaps it was the influence of comparative civilisation, but half way through the afternoon, I suddenly realised that I had had enough. I had achieved more than any sixty two year old had a right to achieve and my rare days of rest and comfort only served to tell me just how weary I was. I did not want the trip to lose its enjoyment – and I had enjoyed it for all the problems – and become just a chore that had to be completed.

We had steak for lunch, but my wasted stomach struggled to get it all down, delicious though it was.

"What is for dinner?" Pierre asked and Kim laughed.

"We were going to have lasagna," she said, "but I shouldn't think David will want to face any more pasta. We'll have a bit of roast pork instead."

I had told them about the monotonous horror of my soup and pasta meals in a mug and appreciated the kindness behind her choice, but the prospect of forcing more good food down later in the day did not fill me with any joy. My stomach just wasn't big enough.

It rained hard during the afternoon and I ensconced myself among the magazines in the camp lounge. A cheerful Ndebele waiter named Nkosana Mpofu encouraged me by saying that I had but three hours walking ahead of me.

"Camp staff walk to Binga for their shopping," he grinned. "It is not far but you must be careful of buffaloes."

I assured him that I would take every care and wondered how correct his estimate of time would prove to be. I reckoned on three days rather than three hours however, as I would not be walking very fast. Besides, he was probably trying to be nice and telling me what he thought I wanted to hear. That has always been the way among rural Africans and it can lead to much dashing of false hopes. I still had the Musumu River to cross which had not entered into my original planning for the trip, but everyone in Sijarira assured me that I would find plenty of available transport there in the form of fishing boats, houseboats and holidaymakers.

"If there is nothing else, you can always hitch a lift in a dugout," Pierre told me cheerfully and I smiled as I remembered Simon and Kenias taking me across the Mwenda all those many moons ago.

Once across the river, I intended to take things very easy and enjoy my last few nights on the road, perhaps wandering into Binga in mid week. That was provided the rain let up.

I left Sijarira well before first light in spite of having enjoyed a very convivial late night. Pierre had regaled us all with tales of his childhood and fearful initiation ceremonies at his private school in South Africa. A big, handsome man, he was a born raconteur and the epitome of the successful professional hunter. I could picture him keeping his hunting clients amused around a roaring camp fire with exciting and beautifully told tales of derring do in the African wilds. There was only one moment that grated on my somewhat raw sensibilities. He was talking about taking clients out over Christmas.

"But surely the hunting season is long over by then, Pierre," I remonstrated gently and he laughed.

"If they will pay, we will take them out at any time," He assured me. "Money is the name of the game nowadays."

I knew that he was right but as one who had been brought up among professional hunters and had always admired them for their integrity and sportsmanship when bringing down wild animals, I couldn't help feeling sad that the ethics of hunting were being so blatantly ignored. What chance did all our wonderful wild life have?

For all that, my day in Sij had been a most enjoyable interlude and I was grateful to the Van Wyks for their hospitality. I walked out of camp long before anyone was up and about, my stomach still full and my throat soothed with early morning coffee from a big urn kept permanently on the go. The rain had stopped but the air was fresh and cool with a hint of dampness. Ideal walking conditions and I rather sourly wondered why I could not have been blessed with such conditions before I was reaching the end of my trip. Smiling at my own unfairness – after all, I had chosen the timing of this walk – I wandered down the beach, around a small headland and back into the bush.

One of my first tasks that morning had been to leave behind the bottle of sterilised water that the Van Wyks had given me to take on my journey. It was a sweet gesture but I much preferred the taste of my lake water and was sure that by now my stomach could cope with any parasites or nasties it might contain. I did accept with pleasure a tin of pears that Ian had liberated from the larder and as I walked along, my mind kept coming back to them.

I have always been particularly partial to tinned pears. When I was a boy living in the wilds of Zimbabwe, they were the biggest treat I could ever have and even now that I lived much of my life in England where such fruit grow freely, I loved nothing better than a tin of pears with a dollop of cream or evaporated milk.

I didn't have any such exotic extras with me and for once I wasn't hungry, but boy I was going to enjoy those pears.

Pierre had warned me that there was very little wild life remaining between Sijarira and Binga so despite Nkosana's warning about buffalo, I walked carelessly and at ease. Another potentially fatal mistake as when approaching a large, leafy bank of foliage, I suddenly realised that there was a remarkably solid looking elephant watching me from behind the leaves. Once again I was lucky and without ever showing himself completely, that elephant watched every move I made to get around him. It was another gentle warning that it was not yet time to relax but I was enjoying myself too much to care.

The Musumu was a much larger river than I had

anticipated. It showed up as a small stream on the maps I had studied before embarking on my venture and I didn't remember it from my rowing trip. Nevertheless, it looked wide and formidable when I emerged on to its Eastern bank. I made camp beneath another massive baobab and sat down on my pack to reflect, relax and enjoy the day.

For all the confident predictions of the folk at Sijarira, I walked a long way up that river before spotting another boat. Even then it was only a dug out and in mid stream so of no use to me although it did give me some encouragement. The shoreline twisted and turned to an alarming degree and I suffered two heavy falls among the rocks, the second one almost giving a heart attack to a quietly feeding rock hyrax. He seemed to be all alone and hadn't been aware of my approach so when I crashed down on to the floor, he leapt high in the air, yelped angrily and took to his heels, screeching invective over his shoulder as he ran.

I walked on, limping badly but cheered by his obvious panic. Served the fellow right for allowing me to sneak up on him.

I was down to my last two pain killers but the gash on my leg was definitely improving. Blood still seeped from the wound but it was red now and not streaked with pus. The skin was no longer hot either and I marvelled inwardly at the job I had done. My parents had always wanted me to study medicine and perhaps I should have followed their advice. I obviously had a flair for surgery and would have made enough money out of the profession to live comfortably rather than punishing my body in outlandish places. The thought made me smile and shake my head.

How much I would have missed had I taken that particular road.

There were two kapenta rigs moored on the near side of a wide inlet, but they were obviously deserted so I walked on. On the far side of the bay, I could see a house-boat so once again I would be able to scrounge a lift in their tender.

It was a pretty bay with a number of shady trees dotted around its perimeter. The sun was hot and I wondered whether I should camp up again and try cross-ing the river on the morrow. The plan had appeal and at one stage, I had my pack half off and was making for a particularly large fig tree when a tiny voice of caution whispered in my brain.

'Remember the Sengwe,' it said. 'You didn't ask for a lift when you had the initial opportunity and it cost you three long, painful days.'

Sighing to myself, I hitched the pack back on to my shoulders and continued walking. A magnificent martial eagle watched disdainfully as I walked right below his tree. I was way beneath his dignity and he didn't deign to move away. Looking up as I passed, I had to admire the raw sense of power in the bird. His wickedly hooked bill, flashing talons and arrogant eyes made him the very picture of Africa at its finest.

A lone Tonga fisherman swung a hand line from his dug out and I stopped for a chat. He was friendly, but almost immediately asked if I had any '*fodjka*' – tobacco. Feeling that I was so close to my destination that I had nothing to lose, I gave him a teeny pinch of the precious stuff and we enjoyed a companionable smoke.

The fisherman told me that I was still a good ten kilo-metres from Musumu fishing camp but if that was so, my friends at Sijarira were hopelessly out of touch. I hesi-tantly asked him if he would paddle me across the river but he pointed to the houseboat and advised me that they were a far better bet.

"Too much *ngwenya* – crocodiles." Flashing a gap-toothed grin he pointed out a number of fairly substantial holes in the hull of his dug out and I saw what he meant.

Much to my delight, I saw on my approach that the houseboat was good old *Abengane*. What a lovely surprise that was. I wasn't hungry, having polished off the entire tin of pears the previous evening, but a comfortable cup of tea or coffee in the shade before heading across the river would be a definite bonus.

Huh! Not for the first time on this trip, I was counting my chickens far too early. As I approached the craft, I spotted a tender approaching from upstream and on board were a party consisting of Dad, Mum Grandad and a youngster of about twelve. They had obviously caught fish and I put a big smile on my face as I approached.

They must have seen me as the shoreline was unclut-tered, but a little to my surprise, they didn't stop to chat or ask what I was doing and where I was going. Instead, they hurried aboard the houseboat and disappeared below, leaving the skipper Temba to moor the tender. He smiled at me, shrugged wordlessly and followed his clients. Walking up under the flaring bow of *Abengane*, I shouted a greeting.

"Hello…. h*odi*….Anyone at home?"

There was no response to my call and I moved even closer to try again. All four clients were in view but they seemed to be avoiding my gaze. The youngster did look at me momentarily then turned away and did something else. Dad looked up when I called again, waved briefly then went back to what he was doing.

This was embarrassing. More than that, it was unheard of in such a situation.

I had dropped my pack on to the ground, but I swung it back on to my shoulders – trying to make it appear light – and moved right around the boat to where they could not fail to see me. Again I called out but although Grandad was facing directly towards me, he merely looked right through me. The others ignored me completely.

It was a horrible situation and I just did not know what to do. This was hardly normal behaviour on the part of Zimbabweans, let alone those on boats or house-boats. This was downright rudeness and I could feel my temper rising with the flush on my face.

Swearing to myself, I turned to move on and to hell with them when Temba's head reappeared over the high bow of *Abengane* and he asked me how my walk was going.

"Fine until now," was my somewhat acerbic reply and I told him that all I wanted was a lift across the 'bloody Musumu.' He went off to talk with his clients and then brought the tender around to where I was standing. Off we went and on the way, Temba told me that this family were particularly rude and unfriendly, even to the boat crew.

"I won't ever go with them again," he said belliger-ently and I had to admit that a week spent cooped up with folk like that was tantamount to torture. They were from Bulawayo too, a city renowned for its friendly hospitality.

⮾

As we puttered across the river, Temba and I set the world to rights and discussed the pleasures of working on a boat like *Abengane*. He had been with the boat for sixteen years, having started as a lowly deckhand and assured me that he could not wish for a better or more cosseted job.

"The owners are very good to me," he said simply. "They look after me and my family very well so I can put up with the occasional bad clients for their sakes."

Temba also pointed out the route I should take after he had dropped me off and told me that I was only a few kilometres from Binga town. When he asked where I was staying, I mentioned the Koks and he told me that I would probably find Bushpig at Musumu Lodge, as he worked for the company that owned the place.

"He likes to drink their vodka and tell stories about the old days," he laughed and I laughed with him. It was incredible to think that I was so close to my old friends and the end of my journey.

I wasn't there yet though. Temba dropped me off beside Musumu fishing camp – it was on the wrong side of the river so I had gone astray again although it didn't seem to matter at that stage – and off I went. It was a long hard walk after a long, hard morning and I could feel the strength draining from my muscles. Drizzle fell steadily and the few Tonga youngsters I passed looked curiously at me but as with all the Tonga I had met along the road, they were too polite to comment or ask what on earth I thought I was doing. Some of the way was over flat ground but much of it was rocky and I fell twice more, bringing my fall tally for that day to five. Taken together with the encounter with the miserable family from Bulawayo, that was enough to make it a particularly bad day, but I was happy. My adventure was almost over.

At one stage, I left the water's edge and walked along a high ridge, but for the first time in a while, found myself battling with thick green jess. This was not what I needed at such a late stage in my trip.

Battered, bleeding and terribly weary I eventually arrived below the lodge and after searching for a path, gave up and pushed my way up an almost precipitous slope through more thick and scratchy bush. Climbing over a small wall I moved sweatily through a barbecue area and into a bar where two very English people were working.

Somewhat hesitantly, I introduced myself and Alan Wheatley raised his eyebrows.

"You must be the chap Martinus told us about," he exclaimed and after remembering that Martinus was my old friend Bushpig, I admitted that I was indeed that very chap. He promptly grabbed a phone on the bar, dialed the Koks' house and moments later, I was speaking to Janice.

"We didn't expect you for a few weeks yet," she told me and I could feel a big lump in my throat at the enormity of what I had achieved. I hadn't expected to be here for a few weeks yet either. It had taken me just sixty nine days to walk nearly twelve hundred kilometres and in the process, I had become the first person to walk around the southern shoreline of Lake Kariba. It is a feat that will probably remain unequalled too as I cannot imagine anyone else of whatever age being foolish enough to want to emulate it.

The next thing I knew, I was bundled into the Wheatleys' truck and driven to the Spar store in Binga where Janice picked me up. I was outside when she arrived, asking the proprietor of 'My Lucky' shoe repairers what he would charge for putting my boots back together, but I followed her into the store. She looked through me for a moment, then did a double take and burst out laughing.

"I thought you were some old tramp in from the hills,' She told me and I had tears in my eyes. "The last time I saw you, you were overweight and smartly dressed. Now look at you. A skinny old scruffpot, dressed in rags. You don't even smell nice."

She said it with a big smile but it seemed like a fitting epitaph to my journey.

CHAPTER SIXTEEN

(Afterwards)

I spent eight delightful days with the Kok family in Binga. Bushpig was as Bushpig always was and we resumed our friendship as though we had been together the previous day rather than not having seen each other in many years. Janice fussed over me and cosseted me like a mother hen and I loved it.

One of the first things she did was provide me with razors and a mirror.

"You aren't leaving here looking like that," she assured me with a twinkle in her eye and I set to on my face with a will. Any man who has shaved off a beard after wearing it for a while will know that the removal leaves one looking ten years younger. I looked forward to the transformation but when that tangled mat of hair had been transferred to a bowl, the face that gazed out at me from the mirror resembled an old and somewhat battered tortoise. There was no flesh left in my cheeks so bones jutted and skin hung loosely. I hurriedly put the mirror away.

Weighing myself produced another shock to my system. I had lost over twenty five kilograms and that was more than a quarter of the body weight I had enjoyed when I started out. No wonder I felt weak and woozy at times. My ribs jutted out and my body seemed to be all bone with very little muscle holding it together. I was a mess yet now that the walk was over, I felt tremendously fit.

Janice also made sure that I ate a lot. Breakfast was fruit because she felt that would allow my tummy time to acclimatise itself. Paw paw, water melons, mangoes and bananas made a lovely start to the day and lunch and dinner were normally stews or roast meat with plenty of potatoes and greenery. There were biscuits with afternoon tea and I made up for all the hungry days by filling myself up at every opportunity. In those eight days, I regained four kilograms of weight and I will always be grateful to Janice and Bush for putting me well on the road to recovery.

I am back in England now and my walk from Kariba to Binga seems part of another existence – even another world. For the second time in my life, I have achieved something that nobody else has managed, but it is all somewhat irrelevant in the greater scheme of things. Nevertheless, it is important to me. Periodic bouts of agonising dysentery remind me of the risks I took on my walk, but the memories will always remain and hopefully keep me going well into my dotage.

They are good memories too. The pain, the frustration, the weariness of body and spirit that I endured were soon forgotten. Now I only remember the nice parts – the roar of distant lions in the evening, the rasp of a leopard after the sun went down; the sunrises and sunsets, a thousand different birds and the massive head of a bull hippopotamus almost under my feet. Baby elephants playing in the dusk on my birthday and the incredible kindness of total strangers live on in my mind. This was what the whole silly adventure was all about.

The only memory that tends to spoil my enjoyment when I look back on my walk is the memory of a thin, sad baby elephant near Mukuyu. Despite the fact that I write on a freelance basis for a National Sunday newspaper here in Britain, my story about those abandoned babies met with a wall of editorial indifference that was very disheartening. In South Africa, I was told not to be naïve.

"The hunting lobby is all powerful here," John Hammil shook his head at my ignorance. "They are one of the largest providers of foreign exchange for this country so you have no chance when you go up against them."

He was probably correct, but I expected a more favourable response when I returned to England. After all, the English are known as a nation of animal lovers. Surely somebody would allow me to take up the cudgels on behalf of Zimbabwe's persecuted elephants? Not a bit of it. The newspapers did not want to know and although I approached a number of other people who should have been interested because they run conservation bodies, my pleas for publicity were ignored. Apart from the Head of the BBC Natural History Unit, Neil Nightingale, most didn't even bother to answer my letters.

Johnny Rodrigues of the Zimbabwe Conservation Task Force did describe the incident in a newsletter and that started a lengthy email correspondence with Ivan Carter.

Initially, he denied being involved in the orphaning of the elephants but when I challenged him to prove this with his hunting reports of the time, the tone of his missives changed. From flat denial, he went to wheedling – 'I thought the Lemons were my friends' – then he blustered and threatened me with legal action should I persist in trying to tell my story. I have pointed out to Ivan that although I cannot say for certain that he was responsible for killing two lactating cows and have never accused him of doing so, the *prima facie* case against him is a strong one. I have also promised that if he will prove his innocence, I will publicly apologise for my suspicions. He has not done that so I can only draw my own conclusions. Although this book is primarily about a personal adventure, it is also an oblique effort to bring the message of conservation and fair play home to every hunter who ignores the ethics of the profession at the expense of innocent animals. The world cannot continue to stand by and allow it.

I probably won't walk around the northern half of Lake Kariba now. That Zambian shore has been largely denuded of wild life and it was the wild life that made my walk so wonderfully unforgettable. It would be nice to say that I had walked around the entire lake but I will leave that for someone else.

In the meantime, I must decide on another challenge to take up before I really am too old. Perhaps it ought to be something slightly less taxing next time. On the other hand.....

THE END

Lightning Source UK Ltd.
Milton Keynes UK

172667UK00001B/12/P